A Treasure Trove Of Rhyme

Edited By Lynsey Evans

First published in Great Britain in 2024 by:

Young Writers
Remus House
Coltsfoot Drive
Peterborough
PE2 9BF
Telephone: 01733 890066
Website: www.youngwriters.co.uk

All Rights Reserved
Book Design by Ashley Janson
© Copyright Contributors 2024
Softback ISBN 978-1-83565-412-5
Printed and bound in the UK by BookPrintingUK
Website: www.bookprintinguk.com
YB0589I

FOREWORD

Welcome Reader, to a world of dreams.

For Young Writers' latest competition, we asked our writers to dig deep into their imagination and create a poem that paints a picture of what they dream of, whether it's a make-believe world full of wonder or their aspirations for the future.

The result is this collection of fantastic poetic verse that covers a whole host of different topics. Let your mind fly away with the fairies to explore the sweet joy of candy lands, join in with a game of fantasy football, or you may even catch a glimpse of a unicorn or another mythical creature. Beware though, because even dreamland has dark corners, so you may turn a page and walk into a nightmare!

Whereas the majority of our writers chose to stick to a free verse style, others gave themselves the challenge of other techniques such as acrostics and rhyming couplets.

Each piece in this collection shows the writers' dedication and imagination – we truly believe that seeing their work in print gives them a well-deserved boost of pride, and inspires them to keep writing, so we hope to see more of their work in the future!

CONTENTS

Alban City School, St Albans

Flo B (10)	1
Ollie Daniel Milner (10)	2
Amber Hopkins (10)	3
India Atkinson (9)	4
Caspar Fisher (9)	5
Esmii Stone (10)	6
Can Konuk (10)	7
Luca Matthews (10)	8
Alice Carvosso (9)	9
Abi Wade (10)	10
Theo Johnson (10)	11
Eliza Bates (10)	12
Mabel Garcia (10)	13
Andrew Chepurnyi (10)	14
Alice Stewart (9)	15
Sava Barnes (10)	16
Dinu Kalansooriya (10)	17
Summer George (10)	18
Vale Rodriguez Mayer (10)	19
Muz Wong (9)	20
Rory Connal (9)	21
Harriet Summers (9)	22
Nancy Hopkins (9)	23
Cam Williams (9)	24
McKinley Currie (9)	25
Sameer Ullah (9)	26
Ananya Patel Parkinson (10)	27
Jago Douglas (9)	28
Eliza O'Donnell Arif (10)	29
Ethan Billington (9)	30
Henry Toyne (9)	31
Sanjana Niranjan (10)	32
Arthur Newbold (10)	33
Mick Yeung (9)	34
Rishi Chatrath (10)	35
Ada Barrett-Pidgeon (9)	36
Jessie Thompson (10)	37
Annabel Kepka (10)	38
Thomas Evans (9)	39
Indigo Cooper (9)	40
Tiago Gomes (10)	41
Skylar-Rose Parker-Neale (9)	42
Kaira Caputo (9)	43
Raine Fung (9)	44
Anna Kwiecien (10)	45
Inaya Coulson-Clarke (9)	46
Lacey-Mae Meah (10)	47
Lottie Hillary-Jones (10)	48
Jishnu Suresh (9)	49
Aurelia Gale (9)	50
Mabel Stanley (10)	51
Hugo Bates (9)	52
Jaydan Shiu (9)	53
Benjamin van Leempoel (9)	54
Azriel Zagoria-Moffet (10)	55
Isla Brown (10)	56

Aldingbourne Primary School, Westergate

Emily Glidewell (11)	57
Rahima Khan (11)	58
Mikey Davies (10)	60
Jacob Renshaw (10)	62
Edward Atkinson (10)	64
Isla Lax (11)	65
Joshua Babonau (10)	66
Matilda Hammond (10)	67
Florence Cousins (11)	68
Eva Johnson (10)	69

Browney Academy, Browney

Eleanor Brack (10)	70
Molly Barker (10)	71
Scarlett Gerrens (10)	72
Sophia Wallace (10)	73
Alyssa Burdis (9)	74
Ava Cummins (9)	76
Archer Lee-Bugby (10)	77
Abigail Hardman (8)	78
Tobias Beaumont Gray (11)	79
Ted Doupe (7)	80
Cerys Brogan (10)	81
Joey Dowler (9)	82
Lily Davison (7)	83
Mischa Barton (9)	84
James Dye (8)	85

Eastriggs Community School, Annan

Bahy Martindale (9)	86
Grayson Casson (9)	87
Charlie Johnstone (9)	88
Kylen Cordley (9)	89
Jessica Williamson (9)	90
Ella-Blossom O'Shea (9)	91
Amy Williamson (9)	92
Aaron Kerr (8)	93
Oscar Jack (9)	94
Kaydan Robison (9)	95
Connor Campbell (9)	96

Holm Primary School, Inverness

Ruby Cowie (8)	97
Lucy MacIver (8)	98
Amelia Brown (8)	99
James Simpson (8)	100
Lachlan Breau (8)	101
Seth Mayers (8)	102
April Murray (8)	103
Eilidh Barr (8)	104
Phoebe MacLeod (8)	105
Georgie MacLeod (8)	106
Jackson Brown (8)	107
Layla Dickson (8)	108
Keir Wyness (8)	109
Lexi McColl (9)	110
Jamie Forbes (8)	111
Lachlan Hamilton (8)	112

Lisbellaw Primary School, Lisbellaw

Caleb Armstrong (8)	113
Rebecca Williams (7)	114
Ellie Harte-McDonnell (8)	115
Archie Graham (8)	116
Lucy Adair (8)	117

Oakridge Junior School, Basingstoke

Rishaan Krishnamurthy (9)	118
Mirha Shoaib (10)	119
Oscar Argent (9)	120
Rebeca David (9)	121
Shiv Lohith Boddeda (10)	122
Vishruth Keshettivar (9)	123
Hrushee Chittari (9)	124
Charlotte Langston (10)	125
Kritigha Singh (10)	126
Kieran Kirui (9)	127
Charlotte Wooldridge (9)	128
Leo Austin (9)	129
Seth Vickers (9)	130
Maizie Searle (10)	131
Rachael Job (9)	132

Old Earth Primary School, Elland

Jack Rhodes (10)	133
Kaitlyn McNamee (11)	134
Juniper Star Bardon-Telfer (11)	136
Hana Amjad (11)	137
Lilly-May Denton (11)	138
Imogen Carroll (10)	139

Seafield Primary School, Seafield

Meg Owen (10)	140
Julia Graczyk (9)	142
Abbie Waugh (10)	144
Niamh Cavanagh (9)	146
Harvey Holt (9)	147
Jake Knox (9)	148
Calla Macdonald (10)	149
Darcey Heap (10)	150
Kyle Buksh (9)	151
Amelia Edge (9)	152
Faith Coull (9)	153
Henry Hutchinson (9)	154
Mason Drummond (9)	155
Isla Roberston (9)	156

Severnbanks Primary School, Lydney

Aafreen Yaafiya Hakkim Badhusha (10)	157
Harley Winstone (11)	158
Mia Morton Averis (11)	160
Bella Mason-Wenn (10)	161
Libby Edwards (10)	162
Megan-Rose Pink (11)	163

St Edward's RC Primary School, Westminster

Valerie Torty (10)	164
Maja Wojtkiewicz (11)	165
Abbey Taguibao (10)	166
Chelsea-Ann Kobla (11)	167
Joud Mohammed (11)	168
Rie-Rie Boyle-Mitchell (11)	169
Khloe Faria (10)	170
Joel Cakoni (10)	171
Nathaniel Zecarias (11)	172
Justin Dela Pena (10)	173
Emmanuel Filomon (10)	174
Kawsar Yassine (10)	175
Kane Bellot (10)	176
Harley Dudziak (11)	177
Fikayo Larmie (10)	178
Jahmyra Jones (10)	179
Sienna O'Dwyer (10)	180
Adam Omar (11)	181

St John's Meads CE Primary School, Eastbourne

Myles Fox-Loader (7)	182
Amelia Tutt (7)	184
Elsie Brown (8)	185
Judah Bloxam (7)	186
Athos Damurakis (8)	187
Maybelle Mercer (7)	188
Jorja Polidano (7)	189
Ruby Rivett (7)	190
Zana Yasar (7)	191
Ella Farley (7)	192
Samuel Aston (8)	193
Dollie Vile (8)	194
Samuel Huff (8)	195
Mila Stoimenova (8)	196
Niamh Macvean (7)	197
Kossay Akalay (8)	198
Jacob Foster (7)	199
Arliyah Smith (8)	200

Witton Middle School, Droitwich

Polly Scott (10)	201
Molly Weston-Smith (12)	202
Isabella Hayes (10)	204
Tilly Morgan (11)	205
Neve Kilminster (9)	206
Emillie Hadley (11)	207
Emilie Hanson (10)	208
Noah Welch (10)	209
Thomas Wright (11)	210

Wiveliscombe Primary School, Wiveliscombe

Flora Leigh-Firbank (9)	211
Summer Harrison (9)	212
Arlo Jennings (8)	213
Stefan Webley (8)	214
Emilia Topps (11)	215
Emerald Samuel (8)	216
Scarlett Harrison (11)	217
Lily Smith (7)	218
Johnson Samuel (10)	219
Isabella Colwill (10)	220
Lyra Burt (8)	221
Freddie Hill (9)	222
Austin Gower (9)	223
Zafiya Lewis Clements (8)	224
Gabriella Haselwood (10)	225
William Wilson-North (8)	226
Phoebe Rollins (7)	227
Connie Ellicott (11)	228
Ella Marshall (8)	229
Archie Flower (7)	230
Robert Ellicott (8)	231
Harry Gummer (9)	232
Isla-Rose Green (9)	233
Ethan Picard-Edwards (7)	234

THE POEMS

A Dream In The Stars

I once had a dream of flying in space,
In my big blue box hurtling at a terrible pace.
From planet to planet, as I danced through the stars,
With no traffic and definitely no cars.
The TARDIS slowly hums as I land in place,
On this isolated planet in the middle of space.
As I walked down the dusty path,
I heard an eerie child-like laugh.
The smell of fear lingered in the whistling air,
Like a horrible truth or dare.
As day turned to night,
There was very little hope of light.
Suddenly, I saw the thing I was most afraid of...
The stony face of the Weeping Angels.
Their soulless eyes stared back at mine.
I felt as if their stony hands reached out to my heart to dine.
As I took one last look at the eerie forest,
With its twisted trees and big purple moon,
Death would face me very soon.
I felt the warm embrace of death meeting my doom!

Flo B (10)
Alban City School, St Albans

My Cat Talked To Me

I went to bed and something touched my leg.
I woke up with a fright and it was really bright.
It was my cat, wearing my hat, eating Pat.
Wait, who's Pat? It doesn't matter.
I slipped out of bed and hurt my head.
It felt like I just read for a trillion hours.
Wait I'm never getting back on that train.
Then my cat said, "Are you okay?"
"No, I'm not okay. Wait, you can talk?"
"Yeah, I can also walk, see."

Am I in a dream?
No of course I can ride a horse.
"How about we get up and get you a cup of water?"
"What slaughter?"
"No not slaughter, water, okay?"

"I still can't believe you're talking to me."
"Yeah, what's happening?"

"Wake up it's time for school."

Ollie Daniel Milner (10)
Alban City School, St Albans

My Fame Dream

Waiting around for my moment to shine
Not feeling nervous, just a little surprised
I've never been in this magical place
Sweet, warm popcorn and an excited expression on my face
As I step onto the humongous stage
The crowd cheers and I'm as light as a page
As I sing, I freeze no more
The world is like an open door
Leading you through to the wildest of things
Screaming, screeching, really anything
The chairs even sway like the sea in the breeze
As I get photographed so much you can't see
My mum turns on the light, saying to me
"Get out of bed, stop being so lazy,"
I think to myself what a night it had been
Waiting for tomorrow's adventures
In my dream.

Amber Hopkins (10)
Alban City School, St Albans

In My Daydream

I'm not asleep, I'm not awake.
How I know, I can see candyfloss clouds out of the window
I run out the door to see what awaits me
Out in the open, finally, a tiger comes up to greet me
Its roar is like wind pushing my hair side to side
Then, out of nowhere, there are wings lifting me up to the beautiful sky!
We get to the kingdom up above
Hoping to see some royalty
Out of the door comes Ellie Simmons, she's the queen of the magical land
Out comes a sword, she's going to knight me
"Do your maths work!" shouts someone
"I'm on top of the world!" I say back
Giggles
It was my maths teacher
Oops.

India Atkinson (9)
Alban City School, St Albans

Video Games

I love video games,
I think they're quite dreamy,
But it's sad when I'm late for school,
Because my mum's eyes are really beamy!

On Monday, I want to play Fortnite,
Tuesday, I want to play it more,
On Wednesday, my head is flat on the desk,
Thursday, I know that they are things I adore!

On Friday, I'm quite happy that it's the weekend,
So Saturday, I play them all day,
And Sunday, time flies by too fast,
So it's probably already May!

When I go to sleep on Sunday,
I think *I have to go to school*,
But look on the bright side,
On Friday I can play and be cool!

Caspar Fisher (9)
Alban City School, St Albans

Once Upon A Dream

There I was,
Trudging through the inky black sky of Wayless Wood,
I closed my eyes, listening to the whispering of the trees,
The fire danced on my fingertips, licking my skin,
It shone among the rough bark of the trees again,
Sulphur yellow this time,
Bright as sunlight itself,
Instead of burning smell, it was sweet and light as if holding air,
With my free hand, I stroked Jink - my tame, horned marten who never left my side,
I was happy,
I was home... home again,
It was true, a fire-eater like myself belonged in Inkworld,
The world of ink and parchment,
But I couldn't help but think of who had helped me...

Esmii Stone (10)
Alban City School, St Albans

The Great Wizard And The Revolting Creatures

Running from the tentacles, avoiding the white light,
Bam! There is another monster in my sight.
What can I do? I don't know how to fly,
They're getting closer and closer.
How could this possibly get better?
As I review my last breath,
I can smell the scent of death.
Bam! A blast comes out of my hands,
As I continue to stand,
And the creatures lie still.
I didn't want to kill!
As the news to my brain gets delivered,
I realise I'm the great wizard.
Oh what I can do with this information.

"Come down breakfast is ready!"

Can Konuk (10)
Alban City School, St Albans

The Planet Explorer

When I go to bed,
The explorer goes in my dreamful head
I imagine she explores planets
I dream she's called Janett
While she flew around in her big red rocket
She slept through three and half quarters of her flight in a snug little pocket
When she got to the planet,
She found candy laid smoothly all over it
So, she gobbled and gobbled
Until it was dark
Then she saw an unusually large planet
With aliens playing catch in the park
But now it's time to go home
Where nothing is unknown
Goodbye for now, it's time to rest
Like a bird sleeping in its nest.

Luca Matthews (10)
Alban City School, St Albans

The Eco Machine

I dream that there could be a machine,
To make this world like new and clean.
As quick as a flash it would zoom through the sky,
Alas, no sadness and no one cries.

The fresh grass on my feet, as beautiful as air,
I tell you, this sensation is finer than any fair.
Everyone dances and shouts, "Yippee!"
Animals stroll and jump in glee.

Trees sway and welcome you to the breeze,
Finally, polar bears don't drown in the sea.

So now, if you please,
Remember our wonderful world,
Also, remember that you just need to believe.

Alice Carvosso (9)
Alban City School, St Albans

My Nightmares

I'm surrounded by endless nothingness
Bang!
My friends appear as fast as lightning strikes
They take a step forward
And another

But just when they're about to reach me
Boom!
I'm in a hot-air balloon, miles above any land
I fall
I squint, terrified of my fate

When I appear to the stranded on an island
As I take a step forward
my feet start to sink downwards
Plummeting to the Earth's core
It's forty degrees

I start to disintegrate
When out of nowhere
I wake up in bed.

Abi Wade (10)
Alban City School, St Albans

Stormy Nightmare

I'm stuck in a dream,
In darkness' lair,
I think it's a nightmare!

Boom!
A lightning bolt as bright as the sun,
Shatters the inky black abyss,
A bolt strikes next to me, *phew!*
That was a near miss!

I hug my teddy a little tighter,
I'm scared, you see,
I'm not exactly a good fighter.

I wish to be back in my room,
Wrapped up tightly as if in a tomb,
When, suddenly, the ground swallows me up,
I scream and scream,
Until I hit my head,
And find myself back in bed.

Theo Johnson (10)
Alban City School, St Albans

Astronaut

A n astronaut sneezed, "*Achoo!*" and saw her magical thoughts around her
S teaming, flaming rockets pierced through the air
T he stars were as peaceful as a waterfall rushing down
R ockets danced, planets pranced
O h no… Here comes the take-off!
N elli the astronaut wandered out of the rocket and advanced to her planet!
A s nervous as could be, she took a step forward, you see
U sain Bolt, her rapid alien, came with Nelli
T he galaxy was as beautiful as a pearl.

Eliza Bates (10)
Alban City School, St Albans

My Brother's Dream

In my bedroom every night,
I dream of flying dynamite,
But suddenly, what is that I see?
Might it?
No, it could not be!

Right before my big, brown eyes,
My white, shiny ceiling lies!
I slowly crawl out of bed,
Ouch!
I step on pencil lead!

Walking over to my bro,
Steps so graceful like a doe.

Wait! I'm falling, falling, falling...
But what is that near me?
No, not flying otters?
Not with *me*!

Or maybe,
Just maybe,
I'm in my brother's dream!

Mabel Garcia (10)
Alban City School, St Albans

Nightmare

N othing can stop the wailing wind from entering my skin,
I n my head I think, *how did I get here in the castle of sin?*
G reen eyes appear in a gleaming corner,
H elp, I think I am stuck in a beaming sauna.
T ragedy the figure is called,
M y god, it's angrily roared.
A pparently, I'm being chased by a thought,
R apidly it's made my brain extremely hot.
E ventually, I wake up in my soft, smiling bed.

Phew! I'm so relieved, it's the end!

Andrew Chepurnyi (10)
Alban City School, St Albans

Wasteland

I was in a creepy place,
I bent down to tie my lace.
Then I heard a roar,
I let out a scream,
I fell into a stream.
Then I looked behind,
And there I found,
A Gigantasaurus on my trail.
It could knock me out with a flick of its tail.
I felt so scared,
I just wanna be cared.
And then I heard another sound,
"Wake up, you're late for school."
Didn't move a muscle
"I'll give you a pound."
So then I jumped out of bed,
And realised it was just a nightmare.

Alice Stewart (9)
Alban City School, St Albans

Wandering Through The Stars

S pace is a desolate place,
P iercing the early dawn light, a flaming rocket escapes the atmosphere,
A ttracting my eyes, planets dance by,
C uriously I watch as we fly through the stratosphere,
E very star shines like a thousand shards of glass.

D reaming of Earth, clouds and grass,
R emembering old memories of home planet friends,
E xciting adventures of old come to an end,
A nother day of being alone,
M aybe this time you'll land at home.

Sava Barnes (10)
Alban City School, St Albans

The Unicorn Island

It's so beautiful on Unicorn Island,
Where you get to ride your own unicorn on the soft sand,
Flying bunnies and crying trolls,
The unicorns listen and start to crawl,
Many multicoloured flying unicorns have a very caring owner,
No one fails, not today, not ever.

If you bond with your unicorn,
You will get your power,
My unicorn really likes flowers,
The trees are made from dark brown chocolate,
And the leaves are curled, bold and round,
The broken heart diamond was lost and found.

Dinu Kalansooriya (10)
Alban City School, St Albans

Winter Magic

W hooshing like a star,
I glide through space.
N ever having a care.
T hen I come across an...
E xtraordinary land where I met a girl, Layla.
R oaring with excitement, it was snowing!

M ajestic; that's what she called them!
A rghh! She screamed as the snow lit up.
G olden; that could only mean one thing.
I ce Queen; that was her, she was ecstatic!
C limbing up the frosted trees and leaping with joy!

Summer George (10)
Alban City School, St Albans

Once Upon A Dream

I wake up and look around,
My feet aren't touching the ground,
I have scaly, beautiful wings,
Which lift me up and up until I find gleaming things.

I wake up and look around,
To my surprise, I see a mouse,
I chase it 'til I see a hound,
And bolt; petrified out of the house.

I wake up and look around,
The clear water feels like a dream
Then I see the biggest sardine,
But I am too full!
Maybe I shouldn't have eaten those magic beans.

Vale Rodriguez Mayer (10)
Alban City School, St Albans

Candyland

In the wonderful world of carefree Candyland,
The surrounding sweets have a fresh aroma,
All of the lollipops grow in the sand,
Sour stripes... unlimited Chroma!

Toffee chewables to the right,
Ice cream palaces to the left,
Chocolate rivers roaring in the sunlight,
The confectionary here, you must accept!

Chocolate eclairs are found everywhere,
Cotton candy clouds dominate the sky,
The wind wooshes in the air,
Welcome to Candyland, give it a try!

Muz Wong (9)
Alban City School, St Albans

Dead

Monsters taking me to the dead
I sleep full of dread
Monsters, dragons galore, I am dead, trembling on the floor
But what is that there, having a war?
Suddenly, I notice the skulls on the floor
I open a door, marshmallows
They're alive, they throw me onto the cold iron floor
"This is the end," I mutter under my breath
I hear laughter, a three-metre figure
It swings a metal scythe
It takes my liver

Wake up, you're late for school!

Rory Connal (9)
Alban City School, St Albans

Imagination

I magination is the key but you have to
M anage it well.
A nger and regret will make it like Hell.
G enerating a nightmare but as well
I magination can be great, just listen.
N ow make a dream,
A nything is fine.
T ry new things for you, can be anything with
I magination. Do not worry, some things are
O minous and sometimes scary but just think
N ice thoughts and all you'll be is happy.

Harriet Summers (9)
Alban City School, St Albans

Meeting Taylor Swift!

The red carpet is rolled out,
Many celebrities walk it in their bedazzling outfits of all kinds,
As Taylor Swift herself walks down the stairs.
Swifties from all over the world cheer and scream,
As their queen smiles and poses for the camera.
She slowly struts over to me;
I shriek and cover my mouth in excitement,
She pulls out her pen and I feel the light touch of it,
As she crafts down her autograph on my shaking arm,
She gives me a hug and off she goes.

Nancy Hopkins (9)
Alban City School, St Albans

My Haunting Nightmare

I have a haunting, exotic nightmare,
Off with a flash, I try to go anywhere,
When I go somewhere, I see it next to me,
Now it's going to kill me like one hundred buzzing bees.

My monster has no legs,
And just looks like a boiled egg,
With one big blood-curdling eye,
I'm scared to splat it in the face with a pie.

My monster hunts little boys,
And steals all their toys.
It taunts little girls,
And takes all their pearls.

Cam Williams (9)
Alban City School, St Albans

The Nightmare

Lying in bed, sweating and shivering
Moving from place to place
I see a tall blue monster with sharp teeth
It's chasing me to a secret base

The base has titanium walls
Red alarms are frantically squealing
The doors will lock on me
I have a terrible feeling

I find a key to escape the secret factory
I can't believe I'm about to get out
Suddenly I wake up with my mum shouting
I'm late for school no doubt.

McKinley Currie (9)
Alban City School, St Albans

Darkness

Darkness surrounds me here
Shadows haunting me
A bear with sharp teeth
Ten long nights and in only one
It comes towards me
Please set me free
I don't want to be jailed in this place
Things haven't been the same since my birthday
I went to Faazar's it was the worst day
Don't wanna start a fight
I'm so sorry that we gave you all a little fright
We're not so scary if you see us in the daylight.

Sameer Ullah (9)
Alban City School, St Albans

Big Wings

As I emerge from my house like a chick coming out from its egg,
I *whoosh* through the sky, I am as light as a fly.
The clouds wave past me, as I go by.
My wings take over me.
I have so many things to see but all I know is I am as busy as a bee.
I touch the clouds with my fingertips.
Though I am hungry and long for some chips.
My hunger takes over me like a pen in a box.
You know what, I am so hungry I could eat an ox!

Ananya Patel Parkinson (10)
Alban City School, St Albans

As I Travel

As I travel, the world goes past,
Like a rocket, it's so fast.

The whistling wind in my ears,
Zooms past me with no fear.

At last, Mount Montague is in my sight,
It stands proud like dynamite.

I climb the mountain with no fright,
As I ascend I turn right.

Down the mountain, I can see,
A wonderful world waiting for me.

So now if you please,
Believe in this dream.

Jago Douglas (9)
Alban City School, St Albans

Shopping Kidnapper

D o you ever feel like someone is watching you
R ight in the centre of a shop?
E verything feels scary like a ghost haunting people.
A t 1:00, my mum was picking me up.
M eanwhile, I was... *Crash!*
I t was a bunch of shopping bags falling over.
N ow a creepy lady took me by her icy, cold hands.
G etting in a car until I hear my hamster in his squeaky wheel.

Eliza O'Donnell Arif (10)
Alban City School, St Albans

Once Upon A Dream

As I touched down on the moon I saw him.
The ice-white surface was crusty and hard.
As I floated towards Mr Spy, the rocket bounced off back home.
As I touched down into the house our tour began.
The siren screamed loudly.
Mr Spy ran off.
Out of the window, I saw Mr Spy being beamed up.
He vanished in a cloud of smoke.
I am now alone with no supplies and no rocket.
How will I survive?

Ethan Billington (9)
Alban City School, St Albans

I Am An Animal

Now I am a tiger,
As nervous as can be,
Monkeys, watch out,
For I fancy a chimpanzee!

Now I am an eagle,
Soaring across the sky,
Err! Get off my head,
You big fat fly!

Now I am a dog,
Pounding my feet,
What's that on my coat?
Is it sleet?

It seems we have met a bend,
But I have one more thing to say,
My friend,
The end.

Henry Toyne (9)
Alban City School, St Albans

Sweet Life

S ometimes, when I lie in bed
W ild pictures fill my head
E veryone has luxury
E specially those sweet treats!
T hey have decorated cookies and sugary candies.

L et alone the candyfloss wool
I nside they have a Mars bar pool!
F inally, when my fantasy finishes
E verywhere I think to live is lavish!

Sanjana Niranjan (10)
Alban City School, St Albans

Mare

I wake up in a different world
Then I hear a tremendous *roar!*
Out of the clouds, a ruby dragon appears
Who lets out bolts of fire
Which come closer and closer
I want to wake but I can't
I start to get hotter, hotter and hotter
And then I realise my bum is on fire
Then it spreads higher and higher
I wake up sweating
It was all a dream.

Arthur Newbold (10)
Alban City School, St Albans

The Nightmare Island

I woke up to a sharp smell of smoke, piercing my nose,
Many claws tried to strike me.
Clicking noises were heard, *where am I? Who knows?*
Obscured, hands grabbed me with greed,
More clouds attempted to eliminate me,
All of a sudden, my vision turned pitch-black,
Now, I thought it was just a dream,
Giggling, I heard,
On the wall, there was a crack...

Mick Yeung (9)
Alban City School, St Albans

Rishi Country

I've discovered a new country,
That I own,
I'm naming it... Rishi Country,
With lots of clones.

It is as thrilling as a funfair,
And it smells like freshly cooked cookies,
It tastes like mints,
I see lots of bookies.

I can hear a distant roaring,
And I can feel trees,
Wait - it is chocolate,
And you only do good deeds.

Rishi Chatrath (10)
Alban City School, St Albans

The Creature

There's a magical creature in a faraway land,
Its clawed feet placed in the soft, golden sand,
Glittering scales swallowed by light,
Wings start beating and it soon takes flight,
Eyes as yellow as a midsummer sun,
It's a beautiful dragon and it's on the run,
Its eyes glare at me, as if to say,
I don't want to be captured now... not today!

Ada Barrett-Pidgeon (9)
Alban City School, St Albans

Once I Had A Dream

Once I had a dream,
Where I was dancing in the gleam of the sun
As bright as a beaming laser.
I could smell lemons freshly picked from the colossal tree.
I could see a little cottage in the far distance.
I could feel the enchanted grass dancing beyond my feet,
Ding! And that was my cue!
My amazing dream was over.
See you next time when I dream!

Jessie Thompson (10)
Alban City School, St Albans

Hope!

I'm in my bed, struggling to sleep.
I close my eyes, just to see.
My cat can fly, my cat can sing!
He is the true one, chasing dreams.
With eyes still closed, I see his warm smile.
"Fear nothing!" he whispers and let's fly.
Sky full of stars, heart full of dreams.
My cat is here to help me see,
That all I have to do is believe.

Annabel Kepka (10)
Alban City School, St Albans

I'm A Famous Footballer

I'm a famous footballer flying through the stands,
My fans wave at me joyfully,
While holding their Coke cans.

I take a shot at goal and it zooms past the line,
But what is that I see?
In the tunnel, there's a picture of me.

Bang!
Then I wake with a startle, and in front of me is my bro Robert Lee.

Thomas Evans (9)
Alban City School, St Albans

Football Time

Football, crowd cheering as tension fills the air.
People still arriving, please beware.
As footballers are taking their place.
Many people are being aced,
With card games I guess.
As the ball gets kicked around,
It screams out loud,
"I'm trying my very best,
Please don't kick me over."
I guess.

Indigo Cooper (9)
Alban City School, St Albans

Moonwalking On The Moon

On a wonderful place called the moon,
Gliding across,
Singing a tune.
What an amazing place this turned out to be,
Millions of stars,
Glistening at me.
Various craters standing tall,
Oh,
Be careful,
Try not to fall!
So much space, spreading wide,
Time to land,
Tomorrow we'll see what I find...

Tiago Gomes (10)
Alban City School, St Albans

The Mushroom Village

In the night, you get tucked up and sleep like a baby, but now the fun begins
I see a sign in the distance, I will follow it, for it's The Mushroom Village
Tap hello
My house is fun and filled with chocolate, candy, and games.
I think I am missing something
Oh I know
Wake up!
We need to go to the village.

Skylar-Rose Parker-Neale (9)
Alban City School, St Albans

My Future Is...

M e and my horse,
Y ou and yours.

F orever and ever,
U ntil the never,
T ogether we ride,
U ntil the night,
R iding at the beach,
E ver so right.

I can't believe my dream will end,
S o bye for now my dreamy friend.

Kaira Caputo (9)
Alban City School, St Albans

Planets

P eople say that our dreams are fake,
L iars... they're true and anyway,
A liens roam my misty lake,
N ever leaving their water kingdom,
E very day, my heart skips a beat,
T he planets are vibrant as they dance past me,
S omeday though, you'll believe me.

Raine Fung (9)
Alban City School, St Albans

Flying Animals

This might sound crazy
But all around me were flying animals in the daylight.
A unicorn went up to me, *neigh*.
Stepping on fluffy clouds,
This was the first time I felt this wonderful.
The unicorn invited me to fly,
Cotton candy clouds.
"Anna, wake up! You're late for school!"

Anna Kwiecien (10)
Alban City School, St Albans

The Void!

When I wake up, I get changed, then I go downstairs,
And eat breakfast, then I grab my shoes and bag,
I open the door and I see blackness,
I step out of the door and I float upwards,
To the school when it is the end of school,
So I jump down to go home and I miss
The jump, then I wake up in my bed.

Inaya Coulson-Clarke (9)
Alban City School, St Albans

Dreams And Nightmares

I'm in cuddly clouds
With galloping horses and dancing fairies
In the sunset light
I was greeted with delight
I joined them.
A whoosh of wind through me
To the floor with black grass
And thick fog.
Out of nowhere came
Red tentacles swooping
And laughing at my face.

Lacey-Mae Meah (10)
Alban City School, St Albans

Time In Space

It's 6:00 in Dreamland,
My feet upon the soft gold sand.
I glimpse some shapes up in the sky,
They gracefully fly, disappearing into the winter sky.

It's 7:00 in Dreamland,
Where the aqua sea washes by,
And I longingly gaze at the horses,
Who smoothly drift and fly.

Lottie Hillary-Jones (10)
Alban City School, St Albans

The Gazing Night Sky

The stars gaze above,
While the children dream below.
The sun stores its light,
When the moon shines bright.
Then I saw a golden angel shining in front of the sky,
We flew swiftly way up high.
We had some awesome adventures together,
And I will always remember this day forever.

Jishnu Suresh (9)
Alban City School, St Albans

The Great Dreams Of The Gallows Of Space

I dream to fly as high as the sky can go,
But nobody knows what the future holds.

The stars are shining as bright as the sun,
I feel so free, as free as a ladybird.

The stars follow me like a cute kitten,
But I am not here and not there.

I am nowhere.

Aurelia Gale (9)
Alban City School, St Albans

Lift-Off

Three, two, one, lift-off...
There it goes,
Where, who knows?
I wish I was on that rocket,
All I have is a little sweet tucked into my pocket,
I wonder what it would be like in space,
Will it be the greatest place?
Who knows?
Sometimes, the great bit goes.

Mabel Stanley (10)
Alban City School, St Albans

Best Dream Ever

Sitting in the football stadium as Usain Bolt strikes the ground,
I'm on the back of a unicorn dancing through the air,
But now it's time for school,
I just remembered we're going to the pool,
But I need to do my homework,
While finishing this poem!

Hugo Bates (9)
Alban City School, St Albans

Amazing Wildlife

I fly and speed through the night sky, and I glide through the world.
I see a cute baby panda curling up in its sleep.
I see a baby fairywren mimicking a cheep.
I see a giraffe munching on a very green leaf.
This amazing world holds amazing wildlife, which I promise to visit again.

Jaydan Shiu (9)
Alban City School, St Albans

Rocket

In the fierce shade of night
A rocket is released
Up, up and up it goes
Flying as fast as a bullet
Whoosh, *wash* the rocket goes
Planets galloping by
Space stroking the rocket
Until *boom*, I'm awake.

Benjamin van Leempoel (9)
Alban City School, St Albans

Glooe

My alien is as cute as a squeeze,
He makes everything easy,
And he sleeps in my tree.

His favourite colour is green,
His favourite foods are chocolate and sweets,
And he always knows how I feel,
And his name is Glooe.

Azriel Zagoria-Moffet (10)
Alban City School, St Albans

Dognapper

A child,
A girl, no a woman
Coming towards me
I try to run but my feet don't move
This is terrible
She's holding something... a cage
I'm a *dog*
"Get up, it's time for school."

Isla Brown (10)
Alban City School, St Albans

Imagine!

Think of a place that you have never imagined before,
A place full of wonder.
Chorus of blue tits,
Friendly surroundings calm you.
Wow!

A door on a tree,
One you know is magical.
Risking what could happen,
You open the enchanting door.
Entering the majestic tree, you stop in wonder.
Wow!

The wonders around you make the room light up with joy.
Cheerful creatures greet you.
Creatures you think aren't real.
Shock fills your body.
Wow!

Emily Glidewell (11)
Aldingbourne Primary School, Westergate

Green Goddess

A woman of grace and beauty,
I realise it is her,
Mother Nature,
Smiling at me with content and compassion,
Inviting me to join her wonder garden,
To show,
Me,
The wonders of her realm,
The colours, the sounds, the scents, the feelings,
She shares with me the secrets concealed in the world.

Her gentle touch, she caresses all wildlife,
As birds echo her content in melodies,
The forests her home, the rivers her veins,
She watches over them with care and love,
And heals them with her warm embrace.

Yet she suffers the wrath of human greed,
Her lungs choked by smoke,
Heart drowned by floods,
Her arms holding dying species,
As she slowly fades away,
Crying out for help and mercy,

Pleading for change and action,
But being returned with hatred and abhorrence.

How she longs for days of harmony,
When her gifts are cherished, not destroyed,
How it hurts to remember times of peace and joy,
When her voice was heard, not silenced.

Will she ever hear the dawn of hope,
When her wounds are healed, not scarred for eternity,
When her love is returned, not rejected,
She looks for allies and supporters,
But,
Finds none.

Rahima Khan (11)
Aldingbourne Primary School, Westergate

A Dream To Remember

One hour, no sound,
Three hours, no sound,
Four teenagers, fear had captured them,
And then the heartbeat drums began,
Slowly creeping around every corner, searching for any sign of life,
A muffled thump noise came from below,
The doors came down, an explosion rumbled,
Gawping,
Eyes wide,
The old treehouse, their only option,
A bloodshot eye,
A bent head,
A plan was formed,
Plans of going to the abandoned school,
Getting there, an impossible mission,
Or so they thought,
Four motorbikes,
Their only plan,
Getting there would be part one,
Finding a place to hide, part two,
A drive, a drive of silence and death.
Reaching the gates felt like a milestone,

Part one complete,
Only thing in their way,
Stairs,
A long climb ahead of them,
Bang,
Bang,
A slow bang coming from the cupboard...

Mikey Davies (10)
Aldingbourne Primary School, Westergate

The Wendigo

I was lost so deep,
Deep in the forest.
Sitting on a stump, my shoes dusty from the debris of leaves.
The night-time breeze made me feel better,
But sometimes made my heart stop.
I could hear a deer,
But it wasn't right,
So I thought I'd take a look around.
And then I found a crumbling brick pathway,
Passing ponds thickened with mud.
But then I saw a giant, flesh-coloured creature,
Rasping its breath as if it was beaten.
It turned around,
Beaming at me with its bloodshot, sunken eyes,
Covered by the shadows of a rotting deer skull over its head.
It screamed a piercing roar,
Loud enough to crack the ground beneath me,
More than it already was.
I ran,
I ran as fast as I could.
It kept chasing me,

Screaming more and more,
And then, in the distance,
I saw a cottage...

Jacob Renshaw (10)
Aldingbourne Primary School, Westergate

The Monster On Mars

Whoosh,
Off we sped,
To the planet of dread,
Mars,
All calmness,
We darted across space,
A distant roar echoed in my ears,
Crash,
We had landed,
Me and my crew crept into the barren terrain,
A sudden tremor shook,
Then,
Out of the powdery sands of doom,
A horrifying beast burst into view,
A slender, serpent-like appearance,
Stubby legs,
Massive jaws,
Razor claws,
It gives chase,
Flash,
They were gone!

Edward Atkinson (10)
Aldingbourne Primary School, Westergate

Magic!

A globe of colour engulfs you,
Flowers bloom.
Indigo skies look down on you,
Clouds overhead,
Tiny white lights float around.
Magic.

You turn a corner and there you see,
A rainbow of flowers.
Magic.
You stroll towards a blinding light,
You hear it calling you,
Calling,
Pulling you in.

The world around you starts to change,
Bushes of flowers turn to stardust.
They swallow you,
Caving in,
Magic.

Isla Lax (11)
Aldingbourne Primary School, Westergate

Unbroken

A boy,
A boy without an imagination.

The night before Once Upon A Dream,
The boy, trembled into bed,
Diving, right into a mess,
Waking up,
A wizard,
A spider wizard,
With a quest,
So close yet so far,
With an action,
Everything changes.

Now with knowledge,
Knowledge no one compared,
With one lecture,
Another quest unfolds,
A mission,
Reaching the stars.

Joshua Babonau (10)
Aldingbourne Primary School, Westergate

My Dreams

Up high into the sky,
Higher than the clouds,
Higher than the birds.
Up, up, up I go into my wildest dreams,
Around me forms a kaleidoscope of colour.
A fantasy, my dreams.
A butterfly like no other.
Wings dipped in paint,
Colours of all kinds.
Wonder,
My nose tingles at the smell,
Sweet and pure.
Feeling more alive every second,
Welcome to my dreams.

Matilda Hammond (10)
Aldingbourne Primary School, Westergate

Beating

Calm,
Silence,
All you can hear is your heart,
Beating,
Beating,
Now you see a vision of green,
Engulfing you,
A soft roar of water makes you prickle with wonder,
Teeming with fish,
Darting,
Weaving,
You dive in,
Struck with awe,
Drowsily,
You float on the crystal azure surface,
Beating,
Beating,
Welcome,
To the Congo Basin.

Florence Cousins (11)
Aldingbourne Primary School, Westergate

Alone

Silent,
Nothing but the gentle lapping of waves,
Muffled screams,
Frightened warriors risking their lives,
Sky coal-black,
Voice not heard,
A girl,
Lying,
Sinking to the bottom of the sea bed,
Falling,
Falling,
Falling,
Until she no longer could,
In her head, memories control her mind,
A single tear,
Terror,
Forgotten forever.

Eva Johnson (10)
Aldingbourne Primary School, Westergate

Insomnia

I really don't know when to not be awake,
I forget the time, I don't even notice,
I promise, I promise, it's an honest mistake.

I only realise when my consciousness breaks,
That the lights should have been off long ago,
I really don't know when to not be awake.

So my dreams smother me like snakes,
For tiredness away me it tows,
I promise, I promise, it's an honest mistake.

I'll try to relax, but my mind begins to quake,
And fizz like a bomb ready to blow,
I really don't know when to not be awake.

Then I'll block my eyes with a pillow, lightweight,
But now of course, the cockerel crows,
I promise, I promise it's an honest mistake.

So then, like always, the alarm I take,
I don't need to wonder why my energy is so low,
I really don't know when to not be awake,
I promise, I promise, it's an honest mistake.

Eleanor Brack (10)
Browney Academy, Browney

Just Dance The Night Away

I climbed the stairs to go to bed,
As I passed the window, I saw a cat on the shed.
I closed my eyes and began to dream,
When the cat waltzed in like he'd got the cream.
He didn't act like the cat I'd seen,
He danced and pranced, then began to preen.
"Would you like to dance?" he said,
I nodded and got out of bed.
He took my hand and tapped his paw,
He magicked us to an extravagant dance floor.
The music began and we started to jive,
The vibrations making me feel alive.
The next time I knew, I began to wake,
"Was that a dream for goodness sake!?"
I looked around, but no cat I saw,
But on the windowsill, was the print of a paw.
Out of the window, on top of the shed,
Was the cat I'd seen on my way to bed.
I'll never be sure of what I've seen,
But I feel like it was more than just a dream.

Molly Barker (10)
Browney Academy, Browney

I Am A Girl, This Is My Game

I am a girl and this is my game,
Being the best I can be, that is my aim.
No matter what, I play my heart out,
Even though so many still doubt.

Every weekend, we play against boys,
When we score, the crowd makes a loud noise.
There is a gasp that comes before the cheer,
How are girls so good? They start to fear,
We wish they didn't underestimate us,
Our play is different, there is no fuss.

We fall down, we brush it off and get back to our feet,
We don't need to prove ourselves, we are here to defeat,
They can't get the ball so they push and kick,
We keep our heads high, that does the trick.

My idols are Mead, Russo, Toone and Bright,
It's more than a game, this is our right.
The tide is turning, and it's about time,
Because I'm a girl and this game is mine.

Scarlett Gerrens (10)
Browney Academy, Browney

The Dream

Once upon a time
There was a girl who was nine
She had a fantastic dream
That she wanted to meet the queen
She loved to travel far and wide
So she could have more time outside
She went to bed and had that dream
That she would meet the queen
She also wanted to wear the crown
So she could tell the whole town
She hasn't been to London once
So she wandered about the city with fuss
She reached the door of the palace
Then she went in but could smell ashes
She thought it was silly, it couldn't be a fire
But it really was, because of a wire
It kept burning until people realised the smoke was rising
She started crying
While her skin was shining
Then she realised she was safe in bed.

Sophia Wallace (10)
Browney Academy, Browney

The Crown Capture

In a land far from here
Stands a woman with no fear
A castle of my very own
Is the place that I call home
Upon my head, I wear a crown
So many jewels it weighs me down
The sky turns black, the air feels cold
Thunder rumbles but the queen is bold
A dark figure starts to rise
I cannot believe my eyes
He reaches out to grab my crown
And swirling smoke is dragging me down
But this queen is brave and strong
I am not frozen for very long
With my sword, I begin to fight
Beating him off with all of my might
The crown jewels fly off in the air
I try to reach but it's not there
The smoke and man fade away
So confusing is this day
The castle begins to flicker
My heart beats so much quicker

It all turns black, I try not to scream
Phew, I'm okay, it was just a dream!

Alyssa Burdis (9)
Browney Academy, Browney

Fantasy Dream

You go to sleep at night, your teddy holds you tight.
Now I'm drifting to sleep, we might take a peep at the dreams we may have.
The candy-looking city looks oh so pretty!
With fizzy strips as rainbows and clouds made of cotton candy.
Please give me land with colourful strands.
See the shop selling Haribo rings and lots of colourful things.
A pool to pick a handful of Skittles, with candy bushes full of candy prickles.
Candy canes pink and white, they even glow in the night.
Trees are covered with icing snow and chocolate coins all over the floor.
People playing all together, wish that this would last forever.
All is not so clear, the world has disappeared; a land of make-believe!

Ava Cummins (9)
Browney Academy, Browney

Frightmare

Every day, every night,
The horror fills me with a fright,
Why? You ask, oh you shall see,
How this nightmare comes to me.
Monsters roaming everywhere,
With purple eyes and yellow hair,
They're coming towards me now at speed,
I shout for help, I plead and plead.
I can see them now, reaching their arms out,
I feel so scared, I start to shout,
"Why are you doing this? Tell me why?"
I feel so lost, I start to cry.
I wake myself up to find I'm in bed,
I can't believe it was all in my head!

Archer Lee-Bugby (10)
Browney Academy, Browney

Football

F un sport to play with your friends.
O n your friend's team until the game ends.
O h, all the positions you could play; midfield, defence, and the rest!
T o the goal and score; it's the best!
B efore you go to the middle of the pitch, you go off and celebrate.
A ll so intense! You can't let them score or the game will end as a draw!
L osing a match, it's very sad and people could get really mad.
L ying on the floor, happy or sad, tired from all the work you've done.

Abigail Hardman (8)
Browney Academy, Browney

The King's Chef

In my mind, when I am old.
I dream of being a chef.
I'd cook for the King,
A banquet piled high
With custard and ruby-red cherry pie.

There is hot smoked salmon
And slow-roasted lamb.
Rich chocolate cake
Sprinkled with sparkling jewels.
And when the King sees my food, he drools!

In my dream, he would make me a knight
For my amazing cooking.
"The best he's ever tasted!"
But what he likes the most
Is boiled egg and soldiers and simple beans on toast!

Tobias Beaumont Gray (11)
Browney Academy, Browney

Bed Bugs

During the day, my dreams are in bed,
But every night they creep into my head.

From under my pillow, they creep and they crawl
Like wriggly bugs, not scary at all!

With hundreds of legs, they tickle my ears.
As they whisper their magic, my dream appears.

About dancing unicorns that sparkle and sing,
And wizards with bright pink dragon wings.

Though grown-ups say, "Don't let bed bugs bite!"
I love my dream bugs stories each night.

Ted Doupe (7)
Browney Academy, Browney

The Bees

The girl, the girl sat in the trees,
She listens to the buzzing bees.

The bees, they buzz, they buzz, they buzz,
While combing their little yellow and black fuzz.

The boy, the boy sees the girl and hops,
Skips and jumps with a little twirl.

The girl, the girls claps and says, "Oh wow!"
"What a show! Come up here and we'll watch the show."

He agrees and climbs the tree and says,
"Oh wow, I can hear the bees."

Cerys Brogan (10)
Browney Academy, Browney

The Snakes' Land

In my dream, I saw a land,
With corn snakes yellow and rattlesnakes black,
I knew that they would not attack.
Because I love snakes and they love me,
This is where I want to be.
They hopped on their surfboards,
With sunglasses on.
One by one they were gone,
I thought it was just a race;
When suddenly, they flew up to space!

Joey Dowler (9)
Browney Academy, Browney

Magical Witches

Five magical witches standing in a forest.
A big black cauldron bubbling with spells.
In goes wiggly worms and long bony frogs' legs.
Now time for the special words,
Witches, witches and furry friends let's all screech and make this spell.
Ha, ha, ha! We are happy now!
You are a mouse!

Lily Davison (7)
Browney Academy, Browney

Dreams

D reaming of you is something I love to do.
R emembering the time I spent with you.
E very night I dream of you.
A nd miss you every time I do.
M e and my brother love you very much.
S leep easy Dad, we miss you lots and lots.

Mischa Barton (9)
Browney Academy, Browney

Dragon Dave

There once was a dragon called Dave.
He lived in a big, big cave.
He hated humans until his friend Uman came and said, "Hey."

Dave said, "Hey go away,"
But Uman ignored Dave because Uman is a clown today.

James Dye (8)
Browney Academy, Browney

Hogwarts

I arrived at Hogwarts as excited as can be.
I saw the Whomping Willow, a violent-natured tree.
Then I met the gamekeeper Hagrid, a half-giant man.
I ran to the Great Hall, my luggage in hand.
I dropped my luggage off while Filch was asleep.
But he heard it fall with a creak.
When I got inside I took a seat.
Then listened to Dumbledore's speech.
I was walking to my dorm, extremely curious.
But then the stairs moved and I was furious!
I decided to explore until I came to the third floor.
I heard a noise and opened the door.
When I stepped inside I immediately ran out.
For inside, was a three-headed dog.
With six eyes and three mouths!
I got to my dorm and lay down in bed.
Not knowing if I was safe.
From the dog with three heads.

Bahy Martindale (9)
Eastriggs Community School, Annan

Scaly Dragons

D eep in a cave,
R aids of scaly patterns.
A gony deep down
G old, I found I couldn't resist.
O ne dragon appeared at first.
N ever thought they ever existed!
S outh I had to go, right down through the cave.

Then the strange ones appeared, maybe this was a bad idea.
Had to dodge around the gap.
What a relief, I'd taken a sign.
Found a car that randomly appeared.
Thought it was ghosts, maybe not.
Hit my head on the wheel.
Knocked out for a while.
Got up and realised I was fine.
Left and right, I was fine.

Grayson Casson (9)
Eastriggs Community School, Annan

Target Wrestling

Beneath the spotlight's piercing glow,
In the squared circle, emotions flow.
The mat a canvas for tales untold,
Wrestlers grapple, fierce and bold.
Echoes of cheers, the roar of the crowd,
Each move scripted yet raw and loud.
A choreography of power and might in the ring,
They dance through the night with passion and skill.
They enthral a symphony of bodies, a wrestling sprawl,
From lock-up to pin a rhythmic trance.
A performance where strength finds its chance.

Charlie Johnstone (9)
Eastriggs Community School, Annan

The Escape!

Once upon a dream,
I sat on the edge of a boat,
Crashing waves,
Scuba-diving gear on, ready with no fear,
I had never gone so deep with no fear,
A talking blob fish appeared,
With a beautiful crown shining like gold, it was very old.
I had to do some tasks to be in the past,
I was lost,
So I got trapped!
I had a cape on,
I had to escape,
I never backed down or gave up,
I finally escaped,
I deserved a treat.

Kylen Cordley (9)
Eastriggs Community School, Annan

Disturbed Sleepover

Amy and Ella arrived!
We had never been more excited!
Even the pillows were bouncing with joy,
But there was this annoying boy,
He kept taking a peek,
Through the crack in the door,
He looked a bit sad,
I felt a bit sad,
He looked again,
Amy and Ella were mad,
He started to walk away,
I held him back,
I even stood on a crack!
He turned around,
Gosh, I was mad!
It was my annoying brother!

Jessica Williamson (9)
Eastriggs Community School, Annan

The Three Besties

Jess is the best,
She came from the West,
And she's wearing a beautiful dress.
Amy is cool,
I met her at school,
She slays the days away.
Ella has style,
She has for a while,
Like the creator of smiles.
We are the best friends in the world,
Like the Powerpuff Girls.
It's great having kind friends,
Not just in my mind.
It feels like a dream tonight,
That shines very bright.

Ella-Blossom O'Shea (9)
Eastriggs Community School, Annan

Disneyland!

In my dream, I went to Disneyland!
Ella was there and she stayed!
Photos at the castle with characters.
Ate snacks, they were tasty!
Enjoyed the roller coasters.
Jack made Ella and I go on one.
Held on for life.
In the end, it was nice.
Merchandise store.
Stitch stuff.
We met Stitch in the end!
I cried.
Next, I was awake in my bed!

Amy Williamson (9)
Eastriggs Community School, Annan

In A Cave

In a cave,
Me and my friend Dave
We were going to scream
When I saw a clown.
Put my head down.
Clown had a frown.
Was in my gown.
Gave my friend Dave a little wave.
Thought it was the end
When the clown got closer.
I noticed that he was very wee.
So, I was safe.
Even though I had no faith.

Aaron Kerr (8)
Eastriggs Community School, Annan

The Football Champion

Once upon a time,
Me and Evan at a football match,
Away we went.
Excited to get there.
Saw the superstar,
His name is Kyogo Furuhashi.
We got a tour.
Hard football, couldn't believe it.
Green pitch so big,
Shiny scoreboard, so shiny, couldn't see.
Huge stadium, can see for miles!

Oscar Jack (9)
Eastriggs Community School, Annan

Boxing

Every night in my dreams,
Flying champions boxing dancing bananas with hats,
with my sister.
I felt sick; I drank too many Fruit Shoots.
And it smelt, but it was fun!
With my mum and dad,
It was the best dream ever!

Kaydan Robison (9)
Eastriggs Community School, Annan

Once Upon A Dream

L ooking outside at the river.
O n the balcony of a hotel.
N o one can see me.
D oughnuts and pancakes.
O range juice with lime.
N ever had this experience before.

Connor Campbell (9)
Eastriggs Community School, Annan

A Dancer's Dream

Once upon a dancer's dream.
There was a little, graceful, imaginative girl.
She loved to dance with unicorns.
One day she went on a walk.
And there was a mysterious door.
She was so tempted to go through it.
So she obviously went through it.
But when she went in the door...
It was the most wonderful place ever.
She had a sweetie house.
And it had a strawberry lace path.
And a candy cane door.
And marshmallow bricks.
But no sign of the unicorn.
So all of it had to come to an end.
So she went home.
But it was sleeping in her bed!
So they had a party.
And they all lived happily ever after.

Ruby Cowie (8)
Holm Primary School, Inverness

A Dream

When the sun sets and your eyes close,
You go off for a doze.
But something waits beyond your sight and
Only comes when your eyes are closed.
You wake up in a magical land,
You see a pegasus waiting for you.
You jump on its back and into the sky.
You fly for a while, having so much fun,
You totally forget about the sun.
When the sunlight creaks from the window,
To the bed, you're still quite a sleepy head.
Someone comes and knocks on your door.
Your dream bubble bursts into the day.
You wake up and say I wonder if I'll ever see it again.

Lucy MacIver (8)
Holm Primary School, Inverness

Once Upon A Dog

Once upon a time, my dog went bad.
Nothing could help him, he kept cutting people's hands.
They were especially mad, at me so took him home.

Unicorn teddy was waiting for him after.
I took him to the vet as he was ill in his bed.
I said, "We've got to know why he's ill."
He then threw up and I came out.

"Did he throw up?" I asked. He said no.
Oh, what is going to happen?
Go and come back tomorrow.
I will tell you the next day.
I went back and he was alright.

Amelia Brown (8)
Holm Primary School, Inverness

Once Upon A Dream

O ne windy night,
N othing was still,
C ats were screaming,
E lephants were trumpeting.

U nder my house's roof,
P eeping in my house's windows,
O ne tiny little boy,
N othing but awake in Dreamland.

A t his door inside his room in his bed

D own under his bed,
R ummaging around,
E ek, he hears,
A t his dream house,
M aybe wondering when his next dream would be.

James Simpson (8)
Holm Primary School, Inverness

A Candy Dream

I had a dream everything was made out of candy.
My house was made of candyfloss.
It smelled like Barbie's house.
I ate my sister because she was a gummy bear.
My hair was as sweet as candy canes.
It was paradise.
Vegetables tasted like cake.
When I walked on the grass I got this sweet feeling.
I was playing at the park.
When I ate it all, it grew back.

Lachlan Breau (8)
Holm Primary School, Inverness

A Jelly Dream

I have a cool house,
It is made of jelly,
It has chocolate powder wallpaper,
And a cupcake roof.
It is the biggest house you or I have ever seen,
But when there's an earthquake it always falls down.
I am so sad when that happens,
And I have to eat more cake,
To give me a sugar rush so I can rebuild it again.

Seth Mayers (8)
Holm Primary School, Inverness

An Animal Dream

Once upon a dream,
There was a girl who dreamed of going to an island
With unicorns, horses – any animal you can think of.
Then one night, she vanished to her dream island.

On her dream island,
There was a waterfall sparkling like diamonds,
Flowers made of candyfloss,
And trees made out of gummy bears.

April Murray (8)
Holm Primary School, Inverness

A Delicious Dream

In Dreamland, everything is made of sweets,
Gingerbread children dance around the trees growing chocolate,
The candy cane rockets whoosh through the cotton candy clouds.
There are cookies as big as cars and as energetic as dogs.
Marshmallow buses and gummy bear bus drivers.
It's amazing in Dreamland.

Eilidh Barr (8)
Holm Primary School, Inverness

A Rainbow Dream

One day, there was a little girl
Who always made her dreams into poems.
One night, she dreamed that the sun was black,
A pig was singing, she was on a unicorn.
The unicorn was flying,
And they saw some flying cats and dogs.
They went to Unicorn World,
And they saw unicorn poo, it was rainbow.

Phoebe MacLeod (8)
Holm Primary School, Inverness

Once Upon A Magical Dream

There was a small island.
The sun was as big as an elephant.
Magical unicorns,
The trees were made of cotton candy.
I saw a flying giraffe and it went to a cave.
A big waterfall and so fast.
A pink jacuzzi and a lot of flowers.
And butterflies so pretty.

Georgie MacLeod (8)
Holm Primary School, Inverness

The Funniest Dragon In The World

The dragon was walking to his castle.
When he got in the castle, he was dancing with his girlfriend.
He went to bed.
The next day, the pizza man arrived;
He opened the door.
He took it in.
When he was about to take a bite,
His girlfriend took the pizza!

Jackson Brown (8)
Holm Primary School, Inverness

Candy Land

Once upon a dream
The sky was as white and shiny as a pearl
The clouds were as soft as cotton candy
The land was made of marshmallows
With trees like chocolate
Everyone smiled with chocolate on their faces
Playing on the strawberry lace swings.

Layla Dickson (8)
Holm Primary School, Inverness

Once Upon A Dream

Once upon a dream,
The family lost their house.
A house as big as a castle
Needed to be built.

It would have a kitchen
To fit a king.
The path would be made of gold,
It would shine like a star.
The door would squeak open.

Keir Wyness (8)
Holm Primary School, Inverness

The Dream Land

It's upside down in Dreamland,
The sky is as green as an emerald;
The floor is covered in clouds.
Birds cheep at our feet and the trees are singing.
And the sun is dancing.
The cows are talking!

Lexi McColl (9)
Holm Primary School, Inverness

Dreamland

My own Dreamland, it's upside down
And made out of sticky toffee
And the trees are upside down
The moon sleeps at night
And the sun sleeps at day
And there is a sky like emeralds.

Jamie Forbes (8)
Holm Primary School, Inverness

Plumber

Once upon a dream,
The family lost their house,
A house as big as a castle.
They needed to beep it.
It'll have a kitchen to fit a king.

Lachlan Hamilton (8)
Holm Primary School, Inverness

Dreamland

D reamland has floating cows in the sky.
R eindeer eat dark chocolate.
E verything in Dreamland is magical.
A crobats can walk upside down.
M agical trees grow golden apples that taste amazing.
L ush green hills get really high.
A nts are giant, they can lift heavy trees.
N othing is impossible in Dreamland.
D eer live in gingerbread houses.

Caleb Armstrong (8)
Lisbellaw Primary School, Lisbellaw

Butterfly

B utterflies appear in the sky,
U nder the leaves, butterflies hide.
T he queen butterfly has rainbow colours.
T hey sparkle in the sky.
E very day, they come into my dreams.
R acing through the sky.
F lying around me.
L ovely and friendly.
Y ou can always see a butterfly in my dreams.

Rebecca Williams (7)
Lisbellaw Primary School, Lisbellaw

Fairies

F airies appear floating in my dreams
A fairy gave me a magical potch
I can fly in the sky now
R espectful fairies live in houses
I went into one of the houses
E verybody was very small
S liding around in their houses.

Ellie Harte-McDonnell (8)
Lisbellaw Primary School, Lisbellaw

Helion

H elion is standing there,
E verything is quiet.
L ightning is here.
I can see fire and black smoke.
O ver me, are two red eyes.
N ow I wake up to realise it was only a dream.

Archie Graham (8)
Lisbellaw Primary School, Lisbellaw

Space

S pace is really nice in my dreams.
P lanets are all over the place.
A good place to find aliens.
C ool places surrounded us.
E xciting times we have floating in space.

Lucy Adair (8)
Lisbellaw Primary School, Lisbellaw

The Mission In The Jungle

Every night, I dream about
The ferocious, abundant jungle
Holding towering trees, and flowing water striders
Anything you could possibly imagine, came in my dreams
I go on incredible missions
All alone by myself
I ripped through plants, with my whetted machete
To crack, perplexing assignments
Once, I went on a quest
Which involved patience and concentration
I thought it was straightforward and lost my composure
To realise I was completely out of zone.
I knew that place was sinister and dangerous
A blob of sweat ran down my face
I could not get to the bottom of where I was
Until I realised, I was in the jaguar's pit
I was trying to hide my reeking odour
But unfortunately, the cougar saw me
She pounced at my face with fury, rage and anger
Immediately I woke up
To see I was safely tucked in bed.

Rishaan Krishnamurthy (9)
Oakridge Junior School, Basingstoke

A Unicorn Dream

In my dreams, every night,
I see unicorns flying with sparkles so bright,
As they fly through the air,
Fantasy kingdoms light up with care,
When all the creatures come out of their homes,
It's time for fun and exploring their world,
As I hop on one's back I think of where to go next,
I have been to the fantasy lake,
I have been to the fantasy river,
I have eaten a fantasy cake,
But today, I am going to the fantasy cave.
I see crystals sparkling so bright,
Mushrooms, herbs, fungi and more,
The more I eat, the more it grows,
And the sweeter it gets,
But... Then I realise it is a dream,
As I hear my alarm clock go *ding, ding, ding,*
Well, that is the end of my unicorn dream.

Mirha Shoaib (10)
Oakridge Junior School, Basingstoke

Taco Man

There once was a hero made of meat,
His cape was flat and round and made of wheat.
Fighting crime like a cop with a sombrero on top,
Taco Man is here, looking after the streets.

Evil Enchilada escaped from his prison.
Hiding in Jalapeño Forest to stay hidden.
But with Taco Man chasing him close behind, his tail;
Enchilada's plan is sure to fail.
"Get away from me? You've got to be kidding!"

Flying up high, wind under his tortilla.
"Ah, ha. Evil Enchilada, I see ya!"
So, he swooped through the trees,
Avoiding the hot jalapeño seeds.
And said, "Nice to meet you! Wouldn't want to be ya!"

Oscar Argent (9)
Oakridge Junior School, Basingstoke

The Weirdest Dream Of All

In the dawn of night,
When there isn't any light,
I heard a door creak;
So I went to have a peek,
Nothing was there.
But then something gave me a scare,
A spider on the wall,
And it wasn't small at all.
The next morning I was confused,
But also amused.
I was in a magazine,
And I started to gleam,
So this surely was a dream.
Then I thought, if this is a dream,
I should wake myself up.
So I went to grab a cup,
I poured in some orange juice,
And then I saw a goose,
I poured the juice on me and said,
"Wake up, wake up, wake up!"
But, when I woke up,
I was holding the cup.

Rebeca David (9)
Oakridge Junior School, Basingstoke

The Unforgettable Encounter

Dragons soar in the sky,
With wings that spread so high.
Their scales shine like gold,
And their eyes are fierce and bold.

They breathe fire and smoke,
And their roar makes the Earth quake.
Their claws are as sharp as knives,
And they guard their treasure with their lives.

In ancient times, they ruled the land,
And their power was vast and grand.
But now they're just a myth,
A legend that we can't forget.

So let's raise our voices high,
And sing a song to the dragon in the sky.
For though they may be gone,
Their memory will live on and on.

Shiv Lohith Boddeda (10)
Oakridge Junior School, Basingstoke

Being A Footballer

F or the goalkeepers and the strikers
O nward to the football matches
O h, how I dream to be a footballer
T o get up on my feet and score a...
B rilliant goal on the pitch with my town
A lthough it's just a dream if I put in hard work...
L ook closely at the pitch and you may see me
L ooking like a star striker
E verybody, every fan eyeing me as I run
R eaching for the football to kick across the pitch.

Vishruth Keshettivar (9)
Oakridge Junior School, Basingstoke

In My Dream World

In my dream world,
I am dreaming about a big laser beaming,
Cackling with pride, no time to hide,
Bullets and more bullets,
Across the sky,
Pain around me,
Who is he?
Yal, cyborgs like we,
Terminator Terminal Number Three,
Earth! Watch out,
Here it comes! Blood!
Now I'm awake,
But afraid,
I have messy hair,
And don't wanna swear,
"Dammit! 10am already!
I am late!
Bruh, I'm doomed!" I said, scared.

Hrushee Chittari (9)
Oakridge Junior School, Basingstoke

I See, I See

I see spiders, I see ghosts,
I see dark, naughty pixies dancing in the night,
I see pirates sailing the deep navy-blue sea,
My eyes start spinning, now I can't see,
Can this nightmare be meant only for me?
I wake up sweating, panting and upset,
My big sister comes to rescue me,
I tell her about the spiders, the ghosts,
The dark, naughty pixies,
And the pirates sailing the sea,
I go back to sleep,
And have a nightmare about monsters instead.

Charlotte Langston (10)
Oakridge Junior School, Basingstoke

Dreaming Hard

Once upon a dream so sweet,
In a world where teddy bears meet,
Magic swirls in a moonbeam light,
Giggles echo in the soft night.

Talking to animals, a friendly sight,
Dance together, oh, what a delight!
Fairies twirl and dragons scheme,
In the land of dreams, a splendid team.

Candy clouds and rainbow streams,
Ice cream mountains, oh, the dreams!
In this realm where laughter's supreme,
Once upon a dream, a whimsical dream.

Kritigha Singh (10)
Oakridge Junior School, Basingstoke

Royalty Writer

R oyalty writing.
O verpowering for the King.
Y elling to think,
A ll the writing.
L ovely book,
T otal helpfulness,
Y elling to help.

W riting for royalty.
R ighting what is wrong.
I t's the royals you're talking to!
T rying to do it,
E xcitedness to win.
R ight is what you think is wrong.

Kieran Kirui (9)
Oakridge Junior School, Basingstoke

Sky Animals

When the moon comes out of hiding,
Bright, bright stars I am riding.
In the sky animals pass by,
Tigers, cats and dogs can fly.
It sounds crazy,
But my pig Maizie climbed Mount Everest...

Squirrels no longer climb trees,
And bears don't steal from bees.
When I wake up in the morning,
I think of my jaguar yawning,
And I know I can always get to my happy place.

Charlotte Wooldridge (9)
Oakridge Junior School, Basingstoke

Man United Is The Best

Man United is the best
All better than the rest

- **F** IFA
- **O** pportunity
- **O** utstanding
- **T** he World Cup
- **B** alanced
- **A** thlete
- **L** oyal
- **L** ife

Put away the fear and strife
You'll win everything,
Even The World Cup!

Leo Austin (9)
Oakridge Junior School, Basingstoke

My New Best Friend

There once was a dinosaur so polite,
He wanted someone to love, not give them a fright.
Along came a boy called Seth,
Who loved him so much,
Who gave him a family with a human touch.
They soon became the bestest of friends,
And went on adventures till the very end.

Seth Vickers (9)
Oakridge Junior School, Basingstoke

All The Bees!

In my dreams, I see bees,
Bees wearing top hats,
Bees holding bats.
Bees wearing ties,
Bees going down slides.
Bees dancing with their knees,
Bees flying in the breeze.
Sometimes in my dreams,
I am the bee!

Maizie Searle (10)
Oakridge Junior School, Basingstoke

Friends And Bends

Friends are like bends, sometimes,
They never end.
They are always there for ups and downs,
Twists and turns,
Through life's crazy
Adventures!

Rachael Job (9)
Oakridge Junior School, Basingstoke

A True Pirate's Dream!

I was on a sturdy boat, sailing the adventurous seas.
I saw a fantasy island with gold shining while what felt like one million degrees!
I realised I was an unbelievable pirate, in my sight,
The beautiful island with the treasure sharp and bright.
I polished the treasure until a different pirate was there
Who drew his sword, looking like he did it daily, I got scared!
But I drew my sword and pointed it bravely!
Soon enough, we were fighting to the death,
But then I got him on the horrible left!
He went to the floor, knocked out.
He was knocked out cold, no doubt.
I received my victorious treasure
But then I woke up, seeing it was a dream I will proudly remember forever!

Jack Rhodes (10)
Old Earth Primary School, Elland

Nightmares

Nightmares aren't always terrifying and scary.
Sometimes people are just a bit too weary.
Nightmares could be like losing a hat,
Or something just as small as that!

Although those ones that are mysterious and dark,
Can often leave an emotional mark.
Flickering through the terrifying dreams,
Nothing is ever as it seems.

Werewolves are lurking in the night,
Waiting for a victim to fright.
Vampires are hunting in the street,
Stalking their prey, just like they're meat.

Spiders spinning their glistening web,
With their eight beady eyes and their dangly legs.
When you wake up in the night,
Scared and lonely after the fright.

Try to imagine a werewolf in a dress,
Or maybe a vampire who is in distress.
If it's spiders that you fear,
Imagine them skating, then they'll disappear.

So close your eyes and curl up tight,
And think happy dreams all through the night.

Kaitlyn McNamee (11)
Old Earth Primary School, Elland

Don't Sleep, Don't Sleep

I'm drifting off
Don't sleep, don't sleep
I'm afraid of the things that crawl and creep
"Oh no!" I cry out but I'm too late
The dream I speak of is like no other
Just wish I was at home under my covers
"I'll never be the same," I cry, I say
"Oh what a shame," I cry out in pain
"Knock knock," says a voice deep inside my head
"Leave me alone, I want to go to bed."
I'm waking up
I'm asleep, I'm asleep
I think deep thoughts as I sigh with relief
"You're so naive..."
"Oh, why won't you leave?"

Juniper Star Bardon-Telfer (11)
Old Earth Primary School, Elland

A Dream To A Nightmare

Everyone has their dreams.
In mine, there's always a light that gleams.
It's so comforting and bright,
It makes me forget about the dark night.
I dream of cute cats,
In a world with no rats.
I dream of being rich,
Then suddenly, I'm falling into a deep ditch.
I wake up with a fright,
Wishing that I had a knight.
Uneasy, I feel,
Realising it wasn't real.
From a dream to a nightmare?
I hug my snuggly bear.
I go back to sleep,
Whilst dreaming of fluffy sheep.

Hana Amjad (11)
Old Earth Primary School, Elland

Nightmare To Dreams

Nightmares are a scary thing.
Many tears, it may bring.
It may feel very real,
So much sleep, it may steal.
A monster, a sound, or a scary clown,
All these things can get you down.
Just try your best,
To get some rest.
Clear your mind of all that you fear,
Maybe then you won't shed a tear.
Blue skies, shiny stars.
Driving around in fast cars.
Think of these amazing things.
The joyful dreams it will bring.

Lilly-May Denton (11)
Old Earth Primary School, Elland

Fairies In Dreamland

F airies are in my Dreamland,
A re they real?
I n my dreams, they come alive.
R eaching out, I can almost touch them.
I s this a magical land I can visit?
E nchanted Land can't quite reach it.
S eeing them majestically glow in the dark; makes me want to join them.

Imogen Carroll (10)
Old Earth Primary School, Elland

Candy Land

I woke up in Candyland.
The clouds are like cotton candy.
The floor is Dairy Milk chocolate.
I was walking around, I met a friend.
He was called toxic waste but not for so long.

He came for me.
His friends are very mean.
One of his friends is called Red Grape.
He is mean, the meanest!
The Kinder Egg told me to run.
So I jumped into the river.
Which was full of hot chocolate.
I was looking like a hot chocolate.
But I got to shower in sour dust.
It got the hot chocolate off me.

I rode the candy cane.
It took me to a restaurant.
I was flying through the sky.
I landed in Candy restaurant.

I ordered noodles.
With Nutella.
And just some syrup.
Just a little bit!
I finished my meal.
I flew back to Candyland, sleeping on a gingerbread.

My marshmallow pillows were comfy.
I woke up and was ready for another day in Candyland.
I took a ship to the dining room.
I got pancakes and marshmallows and syrup.
And waffles with Nutella.
I decided to live there for many years.

Meg Owen (10)
Seafield Primary School, Seafield

My Amazing House

The door is all covered in dripping chocolate
The house is made from Skittles as bricks
It's a rainbow in a dark land
A magnet for those who are lost.

My brother and I had been wandering
For days, weeks and months
An end that will never come
We had both gone to the sea as we were in fear of the darkness
We both had a feeling something was there.

A man at the sea, he was lonely without a care
We thought he was lost
We both wanted to know if he was okay
We went to the man to say hello
And I was brave enough to ask him if he was okay
He said, "Yes."
Me and my brother were thinking if he was telling the truth
So we asked him more questions then he went to our house
He said, "What a wonderful house you have."

Then he showed his house to us
Then we went to the house
The house was very scary
There were webs all over the house
We were in fear
He said not to fear
We said, "Okay."
We weren't safe if he was evil
He looked very scary like a devil.

Julia Graczyk (9)
Seafield Primary School, Seafield

The Life Of A Dog That Lives In The Woods

There was a little white cabin,
Far out in the woods.
The doors were made out of leaves,
With marshmallow fluff all over the roof,
And smores on top.

There was a little dog,
His hair was as black as coal.
His owners abandoned him.
He was left without a soul.

The dog slurped water from
The dripping abandoned door.
Suddenly, there was a big shudder,
The door was cracked in half.

Someone had thrown a stone,
The dog didn't know what to do.
The dog was worried and scared.
The dog stood out of the door.

The snow fell on the poor, wee dog.
One hour later she finally got out of the snow.
Loads of blankets
And got right into the cosy bed.
Then she fell asleep.

There was a wolf in the woods.
Not far away from here with no fur.
She kept sleeping. *Bang!* She woke up.
"Phew!" she thought.

That was only a bad dream... or was it?
The door creaked open...

Abbie Waugh (10)
Seafield Primary School, Seafield

A Magical Dog

Once in my dream,
I saw a magical dog in the sky as I looked up at the stars!
The Moon Dog was delighted to be dancing the cha-cha with his Moon Owner!
The Galaxy Dog and Mars Dog looked at them and felt lonely
They had no one to play with
They had a Sun Friend too but they couldn't see him
Because he was too hot
The Moon Dog was grey and he was made of rocks
And he ate rocks because he was made of rocks

Bang! Then he jumped on my window. He said, "Ouch."
I said, "Um, hi, what are you doing here?
Aren't you supposed to be in the sky?"
"Yes, I am. I am a Moon Dog." Then two others came.
I said, "Why are they there?"
"I'm a Galaxy dog,"
"And I'm the Mars Dog," then they flew back up.

They all became excellent friends
And they all ate rock mallows
They all got hot outfits to see their Sun Friends.

Niamh Cavanagh (9)
Seafield Primary School, Seafield

Turning Into A Shark

I was in my house on Mars, made of Mars bars
With a white chocolate roof and gingerbread windows.
Boom! A humongous UFO with a badge saying
'Kidnappers' swooshed me down with them to Earth.
I could not breathe because we were going so fast.

We landed on a tropical beach
With an ocean as blue as Ibrox, the home to Rangers.
Aliens pushed me, my blood pressure went weird
And then I turned into a shark!
I was a green shark with no teeth just very very very hard gums.
My gums were pink, my tail was huge, as big as my house.

I felt fabulous so I went out to the big blue sea.
After a million trillion years of swimming, I felt hungry.
So I used my ten billion mph speed
And I found a fabulous lush boat called Atlantic Titanic.
I heard screaming from some weird, big, fluffy, purple thing
With rectangular big black eyes.

Harvey Holt (9)
Seafield Primary School, Seafield

To Travel The World

I woke up to my dad waving a lottery ticket in my face.
He was ecstatic as he shouted, "We've won the lottery!"
I told my dad we should travel the world by cruise, "Don't forget it needs to be dog-friendly," I said.
I had already thought of that.
I jumped up and ran through to my mum, Jamie and Rory.
My mum said to me, Rory and Jamie, "You are the luckiest boys in the world."
We all said in unison, "We know we are!" with grins on our faces.
We boarded the boat and waved goodbye to land.
It was better than our wildest dreams.
First, we went to Northern Ireland to see the coast.
Next, we went to Belgium to try the Belgian buns.
Then, we hopped off the cruise in Paris and tried their baguettes.
Finally, Turkey to try the kebabs.
Then I woke… it was a dream.
That was the best dream ever.

Jake Knox (9)
Seafield Primary School, Seafield

The Story Of The Plants

The plants were as scary as a bee
They grew legs and went, "Whee!"
They went to find a rock
But instead, the plants went to the dock
The plants were really silly
So they went and got Billy
Billy didn't know what to do
So he flew away and did a poo
While the whales were shouting, "Whoo!"
He was as loud as a duck
And got covered in muck
The plants were as cold as ice
But when you meet them, they are really nice
The plants went to the theatre
And saw a peculiar creature
They watched a play all day
They went to school and played with clay
But their teacher told them to put it away
They were really sad and thought they were bad
They were really mad so they ran around the class
And they played the drums
So their teacher told them to sit on their bums.

Calla Macdonald (10)
Seafield Primary School, Seafield

Candy Land

In Candyland, I live my best life.
All the plants are sweet snakes and the grass is sugar icicles.
In Candyland, there is a massive amount of sweets.
The trees are lollipops.
The houses are made of gingerbread.
But you don't want to get in...
The Candy Crush, if you do you'll get crushed!

There is a swimming pool of chocolate milk.
There is a Toblerone bike stand.
There are little ducks that play all day and say slay.
Then toddle away as a stray.
"Bye-bye," they cry, then run inside to play on their special slide all day.

Whoooo! Yes!
I'm swimming in a pool of chocolate milk.
What! Wait. Arghh!
I'm sinking, it's rotating, arghh.
Bubble, pop, bubble, pop
Eventually, she died of an overdose of chocolate milk.

Darcey Heap (10)
Seafield Primary School, Seafield

The Haunted World

There's a haunted mansion
Ghosts of dead people are walking the streets,
The sky is as red as an apple
And volcanoes are erupting all over the haunted world,
Vampires live in large dark castle chairs made out of bones,
The haunted world has a leader called Mister Skeleton,
He wears a black suit and tie,
His mansion is as dark as obsidian,
He is holding a vase until he hears a strange noise,
It's a meteorite, the ashes hit the park,
And everyone is sad, especially the children,
They always used to play there,
They tell Mister Skeleton, and he is very angry!
He tells the kids the only way to fix the park is to talk to the magical wizard,
He will make the meteorite vanish and rebuild the park,
I wake up and the park is rebuilt.

Kyle Buksh (9)
Seafield Primary School, Seafield

The Snowflakes

Oh dear, it's snowing with snowflakes.
They're spinning and skipping in circles like a merry-go-round.
I go outside to play in the snow.
The snowflakes ask me to join in.
We go down the streets to play in the deep snow.
We all do snow angels and build snowmen,
With hats, scarves, button eyes, button mouths, and a carrot nose.
We are all going to drink hot chocolate
But they're having chocolate milk
Because they will melt if they have hot chocolate!
The hot chocolate and chocolate milk were incredible,
But it is time to go home.
We are all going home.
I make them a shelter that they can sleep in.
We are going to sleep now.
I wake up and realised that there is no snow
And the snowflakes are gone.

Amelia Edge (9)
Seafield Primary School, Seafield

Faith The Olympian

My dream is to be an Olympic gymnast.
That can flip and make a bang on the floor.
Olympic gymnasts make a whoosh in the air as they flip and do their tricks.
They even get remarkable colourful leotards as they shine like stars in the sky.
The Olympians can do phenomenal flips such as round-off back handspring back tuck.
I know, it's a breathtaking skill.
Gymnastics is an unusually risky sport as you do flips like Simone Biles.
You can get men gymnasts.
They wear fabulous long trousers and lovely colourful catsuits.
They make a loud bang because they are enormously powerful.
The difference between the bars is that the men's bars are made of metal.

Faith Coull (9)
Seafield Primary School, Seafield

Once Upon A Dream

The world dancing, side to side,
In Dreamland and you're dancing
With your friends,
With trees and grass,
And fireworks popping till the end.

With butterflies high up in the sky,
Your dream will never leave you,
And just if you're lucky, really lucky,
Your parents might believe you.

You wake up in your bed,
With covers on your body,
With thoughts dancing through your head.

Your mum rushed up the stairs,
Full of dread,
Shouting at you to get up,
Because everyone else was far, far ahead.

Henry Hutchinson (9)
Seafield Primary School, Seafield

My Dog Spot

I have a white dog called Spot.

He's sometimes white and sometimes not.
There's a patch on his ear that makes him Spot.

He has a tongue that is pink
And he sticks his tongue out when he wants a drink.

My dog is an adventure dog.
I get sticks when he is playing in the woods.

Then my mum comes.
"Mason, stop Spot chewing on your sister's paddling pool!"
The truth is, Spot's a naughty dog!

Mason Drummond (9)
Seafield Primary School, Seafield

Birthday Dream

A birthday is a special time
Tonnes of presents every year, so nothing to fear
Parties dancing in the sky
Or going to a football match, to see your team win
Presents are special... they could be expensive or cheap
It really doesn't matter,
It matters how much love was put into it.

Isla Roberston (9)
Seafield Primary School, Seafield

The Life Of A Table

You think there is no life for a table
But there is one I know
You may think it is sitting near the kitchen
Bathed by a wet cloth

Adored and surrounded by four-legged creatures
Near the window
Called, 'My table'
Having to see smiling people all around me

But imagine what it's like
Being sat on
Or unknown visitors all around you
Or treated like a dumping ground

But imagine boiling bowls of food on your back
Spilled food coming near your face or legs
Your skin covered with a sheet, like an unwelcome coat
If I break, the tools try to mend me anew
If I stay broken, I face a fiery fate

Sometimes separated by my loved owners
Swap places with me – I dare you!
Live a day in my shoes
And then you will know the life of a table.

Aafreen Yaafiya Hakkim Badhusha (10)
Severnbanks Primary School, Lydney

Manchester United

I've followed Man United for many years
I've felt the joy, I've laughed
I've cried, I've shed so many tears
I've seen the highs, I've seen the lows, the good times we had
I've spent my life supporting through all the good and bad

Every football fan will know it hurts when your team loses
You justify the last defeat with questionable excuses.

I saw you win.
I saw you draw
I saw you lose
I saw you score a lot of goals
I saw you lose scores by a lot of goals
I saw you come back
I saw you get comebacked
I saw you winning trophies
I saw you losing trophies
I saw you at your best
I saw you at your worst
But I will...

Never, ever stop supporting this beautiful football club Manchester United.

Harley Winstone (11)
Severnbanks Primary School, Lydney

Reality Of A Dream

I'm left behind,
Even though I am in your mind,
I am always kind,
Whilst everyone is blind,
I need to find
The missing sign,
I am wasting time,
When time only costs a dime,
People push you aside,
And when you have tried,
You have always cried,
I always do my best,
Unlike the rest,
Let me be free,
For as far as you can see in a dream.

Mia Morton Averis (11)
Severnbanks Primary School, Lydney

My Dream About My Patronus

When there is no light,
And nothing in sight,
I cannot see home,
In the unknown.

Except when there is a creature,
So blue and bright,
That leads me home through the night.

It protects me from the dark,
And things that have no heart.

The happiness-consuming creatures flee,
When my Patronus sets me free.

Bella Mason-Wenn (10)
Severnbanks Primary School, Lydney

Liverpool

L iverpool is the best
I don't care about the rest
V ery confident are you all
E very tackle, every ball
R eally try hard to succeed
P assion and skill to proceed
O ther teams can't compare
O ut on the pitch, you're everywhere
L ove you, Liverpool.

Libby Edwards (10)
Severnbanks Primary School, Lydney

The Crow

Somewhere up high in the branches,
On a dark and gloomy night stood
A crow, whistling down the sun,
Waiting for a flock of birds to come,
Down on the ground where a hedgehog sleeps,
Pecks a hungry crow, waiting to eat.

Megan-Rose Pink (11)
Severnbanks Primary School, Lydney

Once Upon A Dream

Once upon a fairy
In a faraway land
Once upon the rainbow sky
From the beach view on the sand
Once upon the Milky Way
In the universe so far
Once upon a little story
That took your mind to Qatar
Once upon a little girl's dream
As pathetic as it may seem
She sat, imagined and went on to say
"If only my dreams hadn't floated away"
Her desires were so near
Yet not within her grasp
And each time she would reach for it
It flickered and swayed like a wasp
So children, think again
While from your dreams, you can gain
And not endure the pain
Of never reaching your dreams again
For an opportunity comes, but don't waste it on selfish gain.

Valerie Torty (10)
St Edward's RC Primary School, Westminster

Steps Beyond: A Dance Of Positivity

As I take a step on the dance stage
All the rage
The caged disappointment
Flushes away
Instead, it changes
Into magic, swirling and twirling all around me.

A portal to realms untold
Through the portal, I hear a whisper of rhymes
And musical secrets to my soul.

As each movement paints a story
My spirit unfolds
A dance of magic, embracing the night
With every pirouette, I break the chains
Transcending limits releasing joyful strains.

My eyes flutter open, a magical state
Negativity fades, replaced by pure light
A wave of positivity, gentle and true
Sweeps through the room, as my dance is through.

Maja Wojtkiewicz (11)
St Edward's RC Primary School, Westminster

Looks Like I'm Not Ready To Be An Adult

As I look into the thought bubble of jobs,
I have a sudden shock on my face.
From one to another, as I choose,
A doctor will be my option.
Then a sudden quietness and darkness come,
Until I get transported to a hospital.
Abbey, your next patient is waiting for you, says one,
Abbey, you will have to do the surgery, says another.
Next option, I say aloud,
Then, I get teleported to the thought bubble of jobs again.
Out of a million choices, I decide to be a babysitter,
Then I get teleported into a house with a baby in my hands.
Oh boy! The baby is crying so much and stinks!
Looks like I'm not ready to be an adult!

Abbey Taguibao (10)
St Edward's RC Primary School, Westminster

Imagine, Dream And Become

I can dream of anything
M aking many things
A gain and again, I dream of things
G uitars, flutes, spaceships and rings
I magine, dream, become
N early, nearly done
E veryone will dream, and everyone will become.

A n astronaut or vet I could be, maybe
N ever mind, I'll be myself
D on't be anything you don't want to be.

B ecause we're all loved
E veryone works hard
C ome on everyone, let's not be scared
O vercome and pass the guard to
M ake
E njoy and become.

Chelsea-Ann Kobla (11)
St Edward's RC Primary School, Westminster

Once Upon A Dream

My feet slowly sank into the squishy sand,
Making me squeal with delight.

I looked up at the blue never-ending sea,
Where the waves were dancing,
Oh, what a splendid sight!

The smell of fish and chips
Lingered heavily through the air,
Making my stomach rumble.

I couldn't wait to get through
The salty-smelling crowd,
Who were all in a jumble.

The sound of seagulls flapped over my head,
Making me duck down, to save my chips!
As I sat down to take my first scrumptious bite,
A horn blew out in the distance, from a ship,
I woke up with a jolt, it was all a dream.

Joud Mohammed (11)
St Edward's RC Primary School, Westminster

Mystical Beach

Come to the beach where the sea is blue,
The fish swim free, and so do you.
Whilst crystals shimmer on the beach,
I brush the sand off my feet.
The ocean is not always the way to go,
But I would say it is a brilliant day to go to the sea.
Children playing in the sand,
Making sandcastles with their hands.
The waves come splashing over your toes,
You just stand still, and away it goes.
The gloomy sea with seagulls to beat, they steal your food,
And mutter that you're rude.
So come to the beach where the sea is blue,
The fish swim free, and so do you.

Rie-Rie Boyle-Mitchell (11)
St Edward's RC Primary School, Westminster

The Deep Dark Woods

Last night,
I was lost,
Lost where no one could be found,
It seemed safe and sound,
Until the darkness came around,
Everyone said the deep, dark woods were forbidden,
But they weren't kidding,
The rain was pouring,
As a storm was forming,
My body started to fear until I saw what amazed me,
There was a hole in the ground,
It was big and round,
The whole floor was broken,
And I froze,
I dropped,
When I was about to hit the ground,
I woke up,
I woke up to reality,
"Oh, that's quite a dream."

Khloe Faria (10)
St Edward's RC Primary School, Westminster

The World Cup

It is that time of the year
The World Cup could be anywhere
One of the most exciting matches of all.

Half-times are awesome
Commercials are great
But the main event
Is what is at stake.

Run a little faster
And make sure to dribble the ball
Because it's time to give it all.

But remember the whole point
That point is to score
and make sure when you do to shout out
Goaaal!

Football is my favourite
My favourite most of all.

Joel Cakoni (10)
St Edward's RC Primary School, Westminster

The Fight Of My Life

There I was in an enormous ring
With two of my opponents staring at me
One looks big, one is small
Maybe I won't win at all
Just imagine I am oh so strong
Maybe then there will be nothing wrong.

Just imagine I turned back
Then my opponent would win
Everyone in the arena looking at me
Now I am starting to clearly see
I am the person who should win that match
Then the golden trophy is ready to snatch.

But what happens next?

Nathaniel Zecarias (11)
St Edward's RC Primary School, Westminster

In Space

I wake up.
I see the stars shining bright.
Flying up like a kite.
I see my dog with me.
At least I have some company.
We stand up to go explore.
And have an adventure upon us.
We both jump high into the sky.
Well, at least my dog has a try.
We also jump from planet to planet.
With endless journeys on each one.
To end the day off, we eat.
Then, have a seat to watch the midnight sky.

Justin Dela Pena (10)
St Edward's RC Primary School, Westminster

Table Tennis

T ables mysteriously fly away
A rithmetic tests on a dog
B alls flying at one hundred miles per hour
L osing and losing, never give up
E ssential tricks up my sleeve.

T est coming soon
E ssential knowledge in my head
N ot a full-mark test
N ot a ninety-nine test
I wake up to find a dream
S uperman flying in the sky.

Emmanuel Filomon (10)
St Edward's RC Primary School, Westminster

Free The People From Palestine

Every night I dream
That I will make the world shine
From the river to the sea
All the children should have the right to be free
From our hearts and above
Palestine should be loved
Every night and day
There should be smiles
That will tell people about their day
Without war, we will live
With war, we will suffer
Until we can't take it any longer.

Kawsar Yassine (10)
St Edward's RC Primary School, Westminster

The Lord And His Amulet

Flying in the ashes
Following Verscio's orders
His glowing amulet
Shining red and gold
Slashing through the sky.

Asking too much of me
I can't take it
I run and run
Rocking, twisting and feeling.

He finds me
We battle and fight
I defeat him
Mastering his amulet
Using it for good.

And it was all a dream...

Kane Bellot (10)
St Edward's RC Primary School, Westminster

Happy Times

H ow many times do I have a dream?
A lways I think
P otentially, I am wrong,
P ossibly, I am right!
Y et I always seem to wake with a theme.

T imes that are happy,
I magination running wild,
M emories I have made,
E xciting times to have,
S leep is fun, what is the next dream to come?

Harley Dudziak (11)
St Edward's RC Primary School, Westminster

My Ultimate Beyblade Journey

My Beyblade that's full of stamina
It runs through the stadium
Like a spiral with fire
It hits and hits and makes a burst and
Makes the best Beyblade to the worst.
To be the best blader, I will do it all!
I launch and launch and get a point
I change and change to find the attack
So that my Beyblade can be able to strike back.

Fikayo Larmie (10)
St Edward's RC Primary School, Westminster

Story Of My Life

The outside is so cold, like ice
I've had to run in to be greeted by mice
The screams are sounding like the mice
But lucky me, I can pop it with a bag of rice.

Twinkle, twinkle little star
You should know who you are
Once you know who you are
Please don't forget to tell me who you are.

Jahmyra Jones (10)
St Edward's RC Primary School, Westminster

Out In The Deep

Out in the deep, seashells grow,
Sprouting from the sand, glistening in the ocean snow,
Out in the deep, jewels grow,
I have a crown, more valuable than anything,
Out in the deep, everything is clear,
No smog or smoke, just clear,
Out in the deep.

Sienna O'Dwyer (10)
St Edward's RC Primary School, Westminster

Space Astronauts

Every time I dream
I see space astronauts.
Flying around, all around,
I catch them drifting around.
I spot them flying by,
Like little flies.
That's what really happens,
When I dream.

Adam Omar (11)
St Edward's RC Primary School, Westminster

The Hullabaloo At The Zoo

One special night when I was asleep,
My dreams took me to the zoo.
And in the zoo, I heard a great big *boo!*

It was a Hullabaloo, that was saying, "Boo!"
And then there was another, "Boo!" Another Hullabaloo!
That made two Hullabaloo saying, "Boo!"

What strange creatures were these Hullabaloo.
They stood taller than me as far up as I could see,
Covered in blue fur and holding a cup of tea!

"Hello," said a Hullabaloo to me, "would you like a cup of tea?"
"A cup of tea?" I said,
"Yes, a cup of tea," replied the other Hullabloo to me,
"Oh," I said. "Yes please."
"Peas?" said the two Hullabaloo,
"No! I said yes please."

The two Hullabaloo looked at each other and said,
"Jee whiz, what a strange creature this boy is."
So there I was, in the zoo,
Drinking tea, with two blue Hullabaloo!

And then hearing a, *"Boo!"*
I suddenly awoke from my dream,
Of drinking tea, with the Hullabaloo in the zoo.

But yet, in my hand, was a cup of tea,
Given to me, by the two, blue, furry Hullabaloo,
That my dreams had taken me to see!

Myles Fox-Loader (7)
St John's Meads CE Primary School, Eastbourne

Dreaming

Slowly drifting off to sleep,
My dreams awake from my slumber.
Off I go to a faraway place,
But it feels like home to me.
I land upon a magical kingdom,
Where all my dreams come true.
Adults behave like children
And run around me too.
Everybody is happy here;
The world appears at peace!
Colour and music are everywhere
And people dance in the street.
The kingdom is a place that really does exist.
The happiest place on Earth you see!
You just need to believe.
So next time you drift off to sleep,
I'll meet you at the castle
Where you can wish upon a star.

Amelia Tutt (7)
St John's Meads CE Primary School, Eastbourne

Life In Candyland

I close my eyes, I lie in bed,
Lots of dreams are in my head.
Lots of colours spin and twirl,
Then I meet a little girl.
The little girl is my best friend Dollie,
Who picks me up in her shopping trolley.
To a faraway place and a monkey we race,
Through the warm, golden sand,
We reach Candyland.
In Candyland, there is a world of treats,
Like chocolate and my favourite sweets.
Suddenly, at the best bit, a bright light comes on,
And with the blink of an eye, all the candy has gone!
I open my eyes and I'm still in bed,
With lots more dreams inside my head.

Elsie Brown (8)
St John's Meads CE Primary School, Eastbourne

Shooting Hoops

Basketball is my favourite sport,
I like to play on the B-ball court,
One day I hope to be MVP,
I'll do this by shooting my threes,
I want to play for the best team,
Lakers, that's my dream,
Kobe Bryant was the man.
He dribbled the ball like no one can,
He's the player, I wanna be like him,
Dunking the balls in the rim,
Watch out because here I come,
I'm going to be the next number one.

Judah Bloxam (7)
St John's Meads CE Primary School, Eastbourne

Out Of This World

In my dreams, I can only see planets.
I am floating in space, darkness is my blanket.
I watch Saturn do hula hoop with his ring.
While having a joyful sing.
Aliens with small funny rainbow-coloured hats.
Standing on Jupiter having a really good chat.
Feeling like I am falling now.
Planets whizzing by.
In a shock sitting up.
I remembered my dream and contentedly sigh.

Athos Damurakis (8)
St John's Meads CE Primary School, Eastbourne

Dream About Swimming

I dream about swimming,
When I'm in my best dreams,
I swirl and swing in sparkling mist,
With my swimming teacher and my loveliest friends,
I swim clockwise and frontwise,
Along the street and the sea,
In my dreams, I went miles and miles long,
About up to France!
I saw all the seasons,
As I swam there,
And it was the loveliest swim I ever had.

Maybelle Mercer (7)
St John's Meads CE Primary School, Eastbourne

Every Night

Every night I go to bed with hope my dreams will fill my head,
As I begin to drift I become as light as a feather,
Floating carelessly above the soft fluffy clouds,
I see magical unicorns dancing everywhere,
And twinkling, shimmering lights in the air,
When I open my eyes I hold onto my dreams tight,
And whisper, "I will see you tonight."

Jorja Polidano (7)
St John's Meads CE Primary School, Eastbourne

Scary Bunnies

I really, really love bunnies
They have very, very soft tummies
But I once had a terrible dream
Which made me wake and scream
There was a storm that was very scary
I saw a bunny with eyes so red and glary
The bunny tried to take hold of me
But I ran and ran and ran.
I had to tell myself I can, I can, I can...
Escape!

Ruby Rivett (7)
St John's Meads CE Primary School, Eastbourne

Magical Dreams

Once I dreamt I could fly high up in the sky,
I was dancing and twirling on pink fluffy clouds swirling,
I jumped on a rainbow and fell on soft snow,
The moon listened and the sun glistened,
Bright stars flew high while Mars said, "Bye, bye,"
Then I woke up in my bed as soft as hay,
Ready to play and start the day.

Zana Yasar (7)
St John's Meads CE Primary School, Eastbourne

Rainbow Friends

There once was a girl
Who had a curl
Her name was Ella Grace
She had a big, smiley face
She went to Dream Land
Found some sand
And that's where she met a fairy
They became best friends
And giggled 'til the end
They spotted a rainbow, high in the sky
And happily, they ate strawberry pie.

Ella Farley (7)
St John's Meads CE Primary School, Eastbourne

My Universe

Under my pillow, I place my hands,
I float into the air and say goodbye to the land,
I rush over Mars and nearly crash into the stars,
My eagle wings are flapping beside me
The moon is so big it's trying to hide me
Suddenly, I blink, my eyes are open,
I'm back on my bed being gently awoken.

Samuel Aston (8)
St John's Meads CE Primary School, Eastbourne

Happiness

H ow I wonder what you are,
A ll around but so far,
P eople gazing,
P eople laughing,
I wonder what you are?
N ight-time comes and I just smile,
E ndless watching goes on for miles,
S tars shine bright,
S tars in the deep dark night.

Dollie Vile (8)
St John's Meads CE Primary School, Eastbourne

My Family

My mummy is the best,
She's better than all the rest.
My dad is bad,
He can get really mad.
My sister is kind,
She has a good mind.
My brother is funny,
His favourite person is Mummy.
And then there is me,
As happy as can be.
And that is everyone in my family.

Samuel Huff (8)
St John's Meads CE Primary School, Eastbourne

Ginger

I love Ginger, my sweet guinea pig.
She is soft, cuddly and not very big.
She eats from my hand and is not scared one bit.
She makes the cutest sounds when she wants to eat.
Ginger, Ginger, you're the cutest pet.
You're the sweetest animal that I've ever met!

Mila Stoimenova (8)
St John's Meads CE Primary School, Eastbourne

My Dream World

D ark, black sky glimmered with pride,
R aring to go, the moon lit up,
E xcitedly a shooting star sped past me,
A new day is drawing closer,
M oving towards our window were some clouds,
S uddenly the sparkly, bright sun came out.

Niamh Macvean (7)
St John's Meads CE Primary School, Eastbourne

To Become The Chosen One

I looked, I shook, and I took the microphone.
I said, "How do you do? My name is Kossay, and I hit 100,000 subscribers."
Mr Beast gave me the reward, and everyone cheered hooray!
When I woke up, I noticed it was a dream.

Kossay Akalay (8)
St John's Meads CE Primary School, Eastbourne

My Winter Dream

Evergreen trees
Icy cars
Frosty air
Smoky breath
Trembling toes
Rosy cheeks
Pantomimes
Snowy days
Winter dreams, so much fun.

Jacob Foster (7)
St John's Meads CE Primary School, Eastbourne

Night

Horses flying in the night sky,
Zooming past people walking by,
Frogs leaping from cloud to cloud
And cows are mooing out loud.

Arliyah Smith (8)
St John's Meads CE Primary School, Eastbourne

Me, The Lion And The Robin

I woke up and saw a lion at my window
With a robin perched on his shoulder
I ran over to them and felt the lion's fur
Which was as soft as the blanket laid on my bed
And climbed on his back
Which was as heavy as a boulder
With a large leap
We flew out the window away from my sleep
We flew into the sky, far up high
We reached an island and landed by
A magical tree surrounded by fairies
Who were all I could see
At last, it was the end of that wonderful night
As we flew back up in the great, dark sky
And I reached my home to my room
Where again I would be all alone
As I drifted back to sleep
I remembered the night that was not a dream.

Polly Scott (10)
Witton Middle School, Droitwich

Once Upon A Dream

A stony-faced school looms above my trembling head,
It's a stormy night and I should be in bed,
Hooded elderly figures creep along the hallway,
A presence follows me slowly but has nothing to say.

As I enter the desolate building through the rusty gate,
A ghostly figure chases me and I realise my fate.
Finger so fleshy, bony and see-through,
A ghostly faded face with a piercing view.

I escape to a cupboard, crowded with brooms,
The haunted figure floats on past, searching other rooms.
Cobwebs crowd the nooks, crannies and corners,
A friendly broom sweeps by, just as scared by the ugly mourners.

A friend to keep me company but not for long as you'll see,
Talons of evil spirits creep slowly through the door, trying to punish me.
A wand appears; my only hope to live!
But spell forgot, there's no hope left to give.

I let the monsters take me although I could have fought,
The nightmare's over now or so that's what I thought.

Molly Weston-Smith (12)
Witton Middle School, Droitwich

The Bus With Wings

Once we saw a bus with wings flying through the sky
I didn't know what to think, my oh my oh my
The dog started barking and Mia started to scream
But Mrs Maliander looked like she was gracefully swimming down a stream
We got on, excited we may seem
It was midnight now what would my mum think about this story of a flying bus and meeting the moon
This was fun
But when I woke up I forgot where I was
That was a dream I will never forget
And now my dream is gone it's time for a rest.

Isabella Hayes (10)
Witton Middle School, Droitwich

My Dream

When I'm tucked up in bed
I dream of people and what they're doing instead
Maybe flying to the moon
Or riding the galaxy
Or maybe even buying a puppy
Sometimes going out shopping or raiding the shelves of the kitchen cupboards.

I dream about going to the moon with my sister
And using our brains that we don't have to win a quiz show.

I dream about lots of things
Before the snoring of my sister brings me to the end of my dreams.

Tilly Morgan (11)
Witton Middle School, Droitwich

Once Upon A Dream

I went to sleep with a blink,
And woke up in a video game
And took a think.
What I thought was I forgot my shopping.
While in Animal Crossing,
I found Tom Nook
Dressed like a cook.
He gave me a quest.
I said I will try my best.
He said to find his son
And I would get given a bun.
I found him!
But with a hurt shin.
I got a bun.
Decided to stay because it was fun.

Neve Kilminster (9)
Witton Middle School, Droitwich

Hoping It Would Come Again

While I was in a dream,
I was blowing off steam,
Hoping it would come again.
I was bouncing off walls with bunnies and all,
Hoping we would meet again.
We were dancing, singing and winning with each other as a team,
When I leaned and turned over in bed,
Once and for all and over again,
All while it was in my head.
Hoping it would come again.

Emillie Hadley (11)
Witton Middle School, Droitwich

Dancing Fairies

I went to sleep
And my dream was about
Dancing fairies with my friends.
Fairies came up to me and said,
"Come dance with us! Let's have some fun!"
So off I went, dancing with them.
Soon, I needed a drink. He gave me a potion.
It tasted amazing and gave me energy to dance.
I woke up. It was all over...

Emilie Hanson (10)
Witton Middle School, Droitwich

Have A Fish

D oing bad becomes a fish
R ush into a wall but have a ball
E very day I feel pain in my brain
A fter that, I will eat a hurricane
M eet me at the end of the candy canes.

Noah Welch (10)
Witton Middle School, Droitwich

Dream

D oing anything that I want.
R ealms, castles, dragons,
E ating puddings galore!
A nd skiing underwater,
M eeting a talking fish.

Thomas Wright (11)
Witton Middle School, Droitwich

A Nightmare Or A Dream?

In my dreams, I have the wings of a golden eagle,
My eyes meet my favourite motorbike rider,
He rides a dragon that transforms into a flying bike,
Rising from the sky beneath the twinkling stars.
Then, bright fireworks explode,
The stars vanish.
The dream becomes a nightmare...
The rider and his bike turn into a fierce two-headed dragon,
Its glowing red eyes like embers,
My eyes search for the ground,
But to my horror, the land is a sea,
A sea of fat hairy tarantulas!
All of a sudden my wings detach from my back,
Foul-smelling winds whip my face,
My back hits something hard,
The grimy, wooden deck of a pirate ship,
I stand and try to let out a battle cry but my voice is gone!
Cutlasses clash,
So I jump,
It becomes too much to bear,
My eyes flick open.

Flora Leigh-Firbank (9)
Wiveliscombe Primary School, Wiveliscombe

The Midnight Sky

Once there was a cat,
Who always sat on his doorstep mat.
But then up above he saw a fight,
So he got a kite and then he might.
Fly into the midnight sky,
When he was there, he saw it was a fair.
It was a stallion and a mare,
He wanted her to marry him.
But she said, "I don't like the name, Tim."
The cat told them to go apart,
The mare decided to do some art.
And the stallion sorted out his mind,
The cat was happy that the stars were now kind.
Instead of bullies, which they were before,
The cat named himself Midnight, even though he wanted more.
Midnight soared down and down on his kite.
He got there before the second night.
So down he settled down on his mat,
The stars all said, "Hooray for the King Cat!"

Summer Harrison (9)
Wiveliscombe Primary School, Wiveliscombe

Dad Is The Best

D ad is my favourite and always will be
A dad who does everything, especially for me
D riving us around to football and the best places

I n my dreams, he makes really good funny faces
S lowly drifting off to sleep, he gives kisses and cuddles

T he best dad ever that does lots of fun football puzzles
H e and I have so much fun on his birthday
E asily go to bed and the next day we will play

B etsie plays football with me and Dad and we are very glad
E pic Dad is forty and that's definitely not bad
S ometimes Dad goes, he will come back and I play with Mum
T he time we spend together, it is really, really good fun.

Arlo Jennings (8)
Wiveliscombe Primary School, Wiveliscombe

Mystical Wizards

Mystical wizards hiding in the corner of the shed,
The mystical wizards haven't been fed,
So they went to the yard,
But all they could find was lard,
It was twelve o'clock so the clocks went chime,
But all they could find was a lime,
Soon the clocks struck three,
The wizards called,
"We need to be fed or there'll be trouble ahead,"
Then the clock rang for four and they didn't seem very poor,
They had some crumbs but they needed more,
Next, the clock chimed six
And they returned to bed for the night ahead,
But they found a mouse in the corner of the house,
And having been fed, they went to bed.

Stefan Webley (8)
Wiveliscombe Primary School, Wiveliscombe

Me And Mary!

When I close my eyes,
I'm pulled into a world of fairies and spies,
Last night was different though,

I looked up to see,
Black Ven staring back at me,
And Mary Anning doing so too,

She helped me up,
And she gave me a hammer,
I didn't stammer,

We looked for something big,
So we carried on the dig,
Then I found something huge, part of a monster,

But I didn't get to finish my dream
Me and Mary are no longer a team,
As it is time to get up for school.

Emilia Topps (11)
Wiveliscombe Primary School, Wiveliscombe

My Love For Gymnastics

G ymnastics is freedom,
Y oung and old.
M ajor achievements and mistakes are proof you're trying.
N atural skills,
A ge doesn't matter.
S till going,
T aking pride.
I t's not about winning or losing,
C ourageous and confident looks on faces.
S o hopeful to make it.

Where you flip in the sky,
And make a better spy.
Cartwheel and elbow stand,
Up so high.
Shining in sight,
As I tumbled into the sky.

Emerald Samuel (8)
Wiveliscombe Primary School, Wiveliscombe

The Endless Wild

The night had come,
It had to be done;
Venturing into the wild, wondrous wood,
Only I could,
Make this decision to enter it,
Although this was a bit,
Wild!

The endless wild crunching,
The endless wild hunching,
Of my shoulders,
Millions of huge boulders.
My comfort was only a cave,
I must have been very brave.

A thumping heart I felt,
What if I could melt?
I would be back,
In bed, safe and sound.
I then woke not remembering a thing.

Scarlett Harrison (11)
Wiveliscombe Primary School, Wiveliscombe

Gymnastics

G old medal, well done!
Y ou are the overall competition winner for age 7.
M edals hanging around my neck, *clitter clatter!*
N ew leotard, covered in shiny gems.
A erial into backward walkover, completed perfectly.
S ide splits all the way to the floor.
T umble track, very bouncy; makes me flip high!
I love swinging around and around on the bars.
C oach is cheering me on!
S tretch and yawn, it was all a dream.

Lily Smith (7)
Wiveliscombe Primary School, Wiveliscombe

Every Night In My Dreams

Shining up high comes a different dream,
But as for me, I come with a dream full of light, peace and success,
As stars glitter, I shine,
Hoping to bring happiness to your dreams,
My dream of becoming a footballer,
Working daily to be the world-class star,
Bringing happiness into the team of eleven,
We hit, run and pass through the grass,
We play on the mud and grass,
While having crazy hopes,
Wishing on shooting stars,
To make us the best we can be.

Johnson Samuel (10)
Wiveliscombe Primary School, Wiveliscombe

Dreamers

D reamers, oh dreamers, there are only a few,
R oaring and pouncing in their dreams without needing the loo,
E very day closing their eyes and opening a new book,
A nd in every dream, they take a good look,
M any wish they could be a dreamer however, it is only the people who let their imaginations run wild and,
E njoy food that is mild,
R acing to become the top dreamer,
S o they become a great beamer.

Isabella Colwill (10)
Wiveliscombe Primary School, Wiveliscombe

A Moonlit Ride

Every night, I can see,
A beautiful pegasus in my dream.
It flies so high,
And lights up the sky.
Its colours are bright
And it glides like a kite.
Suddenly, the pegasus comes near
And I realise I have nothing to fear.
I climb on its back
And her wings start to flap.
I feel so free
As I grip with my knee.
But when I wake,
I find it's fake.
Just another dream
That I have seen.

Lyra Burt (8)
Wiveliscombe Primary School, Wiveliscombe

Spiders

Silky webs entombing its prey,
Who knows what it's capable of when its eggs are at stake,
Moving more swiftly than a soaring butterfly,
Sucking the blood out of pesky flies,
Enormous tarantulas make your skin crawl like you're on fire,
Small ones make your blood go cold as they scuttle towards you at a frightful pace,
But inevitably they are there for a reason,
To catch those annoying flies.

Freddie Hill (9)
Wiveliscombe Primary School, Wiveliscombe

Worrying

For Auntie Katie

W icked monsters peer into my imagination
O ver and over they break my concentration
R acing feelings never slow down
R eady to give up as my thoughts never drown
Y ou spot me in the corner struggling to cope
I nstantly your smile gives me hope
N ever in my lifetime did I think I'd find such a friend
G ratitude and love I will give you to the end.

Austin Gower (9)
Wiveliscombe Primary School, Wiveliscombe

Flying High

Flying high across the sky, candyfloss clouds are flashing by
On my glamourous white-winged steed
The most exquisite of his breed
The clouds have parted far below
I peer down which only shows
A tiny emerald in the sea
A magic place just for me
Down and down until we land
To join the mermaids on the sand
Together we swim and play
Then I wake and find it's day!

Zafiya Lewis Clements (8)
Wiveliscombe Primary School, Wiveliscombe

Tornado

T onight, sleepy, getting in my bed,
O verwhelming thoughts running through my head,
R emembering the nightmare I've previously had,
N othing is wrong so why am I sad?
A ll of a sudden, frightening to see,
D arkness and clouds that are whirling around me,
O pen my eyes and the sadness has gone, the sun has come out, and I see my mum.

Gabriella Haselwood (10)
Wiveliscombe Primary School, Wiveliscombe

Nightmares

N ightmares are the ones you don't like,
I ncredible things that happen at night,
G et it out of your head,
H orrible dreams that you can't stop,
T remendously bad,
M ost nightmares are evil,
A wful things happen in your head,
R ather regret,
E ager to stop but you can't,
S o annoying.

William Wilson-North (8)
Wiveliscombe Primary School, Wiveliscombe

In My Dream

In my dream, I saw a stream,
That led one to a light beam,
I saw the stars up above,
Suddenly a pegasus appeared, flying high,
Lighting up the sky like a kite,
It came near, I climbed on its back, amazed,
As I dozed off to sleep in my dream and woke up,
Staring at the dazzling sun in a new world,
But realised it was just a dream that had been the future.

Phoebe Rollins (7)
Wiveliscombe Primary School, Wiveliscombe

My Dreams

My dreams always change,
They switch, move and range,
Sometimes I'll be a princess in a palace,
And sometimes I'll be in Wonderland dressed up as Alice,
Maybe I'm a traveller looking at all the sights to see,
Or maybe I'm just me,
I'll trek through dangerous woods,
Fly into neighbourhoods,
But when the nightmares come through my head,
I know I'm nice and warm in bed.

Connie Ellicott (11)
Wiveliscombe Primary School, Wiveliscombe

Imagination

I magination is amazing
M akes your brain whirr
A dream can take flight
G ood things or bad
I n a world of your own
N ever stop dreaming
A new Neverland
T ime seems to freeze
I n your mind
O nly you decide what happens next
N othing can stop you.

Ella Marshall (8)
Wiveliscombe Primary School, Wiveliscombe

Wizard

W izards can make blizzards
I saw a wizard turn a mouse into a lizard
Z ooming through the night on a bright broomstick
A wizard can turn a cat into a stick
R acing through the night
D oing mischievous stuff in your sight.

Archie Flower (7)
Wiveliscombe Primary School, Wiveliscombe

My Dream

D oing sports makes me feel happy.
R unners all around me.
E verything was blurry because I was going so fast.
A thletics is very fun to me.
M y dream is to be a champion athlete.

Robert Ellicott (8)
Wiveliscombe Primary School, Wiveliscombe

As Everything Nice

As silly as fun,
As royal as a queen,
As buzzy as a bee,
As stealthy as a tiger,
Smooth as a glider,
As sweet as sugar
And everything nice,
As straight as a line, and
As old as time.

Harry Gummer (9)
Wiveliscombe Primary School, Wiveliscombe

Dance

Every night,
They appear in my sight,
With colours beaming so bright,
Just into the light,
As they dance in the room,
I can't help but zoom,
With my shoes on,
I am ready to go on.

Isla-Rose Green (9)
Wiveliscombe Primary School, Wiveliscombe

Beach

B lue skies are above me.
E very day I go here.
A rchery, over there!
"**C** an I go?" I ask my mum.
H ome, I am going. I have my favourite teddy here!

Ethan Picard-Edwards (7)
Wiveliscombe Primary School, Wiveliscombe

YOUNG WRITERS INFORMATION

We hope you have enjoyed reading this book – and that you will continue to in the coming years.

If you're a young writer who enjoys reading and creative writing, or the parent of an enthusiastic poet or story writer, do visit our website **www.youngwriters.co.uk**. Here you will find free competitions, workshops and games, as well as recommended reads, a poetry glossary and our blog.

If you would like to order further copies of this book, or any of our other titles, then please give us a call or visit **www.youngwriters.co.uk**.

Young Writers
Remus House
Coltsfoot Drive
Peterborough
PE2 9BF
(01733) 890066
info@youngwriters.co.uk

YoungWritersUK   **YoungWritersCW**
youngwriterscw   **youngwriterscw**